farm-to-table desserts

farm-to-table desserts

80 SEASONAL, ORGANIC RECIPES MADE FROM YOUR LOCAL FARMERS' MARKET

lei shishak

AUTHOR OF *BEACH HOUSE BAKING* AND *BEACH HOUSE BRUNCH*

Skyhorse Publishing

Skyhorse Publishing books may be purchased in bulk at special discounts for sales promotion, corporate gifts, fund-raising, or educational purposes. Special editions can also be created to specifications. For details, contact the Special Sales Department, Skyhorse Publishing, 307 West 36th Street, 11th Floor, New York, NY 10018 or info@skyhorsepublishing.com.

Skyhorse® and Skyhorse Publishing® are registered trademarks of Skyhorse Publishing, Inc.®, a Delaware corporation.

Visit our website at www.skyhorsepublishing.com.

10 9 8 7 6 5 4 3 2 1

Library of Congress Cataloging-in-Publication Data is available on file.

Cover design by Jenny Zemanek
Cover photo by Alan De Herrera

Print ISBN: 978-1-5107-1692-6
Ebook ISBN: 978-1-5107-1693-3

Printed in China

For G.
You had me at "Who's the kid?"

Table of Contents

Introduction

It is now more important than ever to seek out organically grown, seasonal produce where we live. Too many of our local farms are being trampled on by the heavy foot of large agribusiness conglomerates. When we shop at farmers' markets, we support our local economy and invest money back into our community. We put food into our bodies that is healthier, tastier, and packed with essential nutrients specific to the environment near where we live. It is the freshest and most vital produce around. Oftentimes, produce found at farmers' markets are literally picked hours before they're sold.

Growing up in rural Pennsylvania, my family and I would visit nearby farms where many farmers had roadside stands with fresh fruit, eggs, produce, and other just-picked items. I was so fortunate to grow up in this environment where fresh produce was readily available. In *Farm-to-Table Desserts*, I share favorite recipes inspired by my local farmers' markets in southern California where I now reside. Every week I discover what's in season and spend the afternoon turning my finds into mouthwatering, delicious desserts. Creating simple desserts using ingredients at their prime is what I love to do the most, and I hope this book inspires you to do the same.

In this book, you'll notice the recipes are separated into chapters corresponding to each of the four seasons. Each chapter begins with a list of fruits and vegetables that are in season during those months. Since there are some fruits and vegetables that cross seasons, you will find them listed in multiple chapters. Please also note that these lists are not comprehensive but rather a selection of common produce.

While all the recipes in this book are near and dear to my heart, some of my favorites include Peach Cobbler, White Fig Slab Pie, Sweet Corn Panna Cotta, Strawberry Hand Pies, Ruby Red Grapefruit Pie, and Blueberry Zeppoles. Buying locally sourced, organic ingredients is a satisfying way to bake that, once started, becomes an easy habit. Before you know it, you'll be baking seasonally, locally, and organically all year long.

Why Farmers' Markets

Let's start with the benefits to us, the consumer, because there are *so* many. If you have never been to a farmers' market, you are missing out on a vast selection of unique produce as well as the plethora of heirloom varieties that exist. We are all familiar with the orange carrots found in grocery stores, but did you know that they come in different shapes and colors ranging from white, yellow, red, to purple? We also know the common Red Delicious, Fuji, and Macintosh apples, but did you know there are over 2,000 varieties in the US alone including the Lady Alice, Aurora, Stayman, and Arkansas Black? It's when you go to your local farmers' market that you discover the many different types of fruits and vegetables that are grown where you live.

Farmers' markets also give you the opportunity to build relationships with your local farmers by speaking with them directly. You can ask them questions about how their produce is grown and get ideas for the best way to cook and bake with them. Likewise, markets are a great place to meet your neighbors, catch up with friends, and experience a community gathering since markets are the heart of many towns. Let's not forget that shopping at the market is also a great way to get outside and exercise. Bring along your reusable shopping bag and I guarantee that within minutes it will be stuffed with produce, making it a formidable weight that will exercise your arm muscles!

The economics of farmers' markets directly benefit you as well; shopping at them keeps money in your community and helps to preserve and create local jobs. Your neighborhood will continue to thrive and grow, and the person you hand your money to played a part in making or growing that item. How awesome is that?

Studies show that produce begins to lose its nutritional value soon after it is harvested and continues to decline as time elapses. Let's imagine how long the produce found at grocery stores has been sitting on the shelves since being harvested; likely days, right? On the flipside, produce at farmers' markets is at your fingertips within hours of being harvested. Picked at their peak of freshness, they have the highest possible amount of vitamins and minerals. They taste better and are better for you.

There is a big push these days to eat organic, non-GMO items, and much of the produce at farmers' markets fits the bill. These items are better for you and the environment. Plus, eating healthier today may end up saving you future health care costs. Likewise, eating seasonally has shown to be a healthier way of life. Since you'll only find in-season produce at farmers' markets, you'll have no problem sticking to a seasonal and healthy diet.

Now that we know how we benefit from shopping at farmers' markets, let's talk about how the farmers benefit. Mainly, there is a huge financial benefit to farmers by selling directly to you, the customer. Farmers' markets allow them to forego using and paying a middleman (a.k.a. food broker) to distribute and sell their produce. They don't have to utilize refrigeration and storage facilities that can cost a lot of money; rather, they harvest their produce and take their goods straight to the markets. Money comes in directly from the consumer, into their hands, and invested back into their farms and communities.

Farmers, like any creative artist, take pride in their work. They want you to experience eating their produce at its peak freshness and taste. So when you buy an apple from a farmer and swoon over how delicious it is, it's so much more rewarding for them than handing over their apples to a large distributor.

A Little History

Most archival sources credit Boston, Massachusetts as being home to the first US farmers' market in 1634. Today, there are over 8,600 markets across the United States with the most located in California and New York. A list of national farmers' markets can be found on the USDA website.*

---

*www.ams.usda.gov/local-food-irectories/farmersmarkets

Why Organic

Not very long ago, buying organic foods required a real effort to find farmers raising their crops and livestock without chemicals, antibiotics, or genetic modification. Consumers had few choices, mainly consisting of farmers' markets and a few natural food stores. Supermarket chains weren't an option as their production volumes increased to meet the expanding consumer needs for lower prices and greater quantity. Large farms grew even larger and leveraged anything they could to ensure higher yields, longer shelf life, and resistance to damage and disease. Small farms came under greater pressure to expand or sell to the point where making money raising and selling organic products became almost impossible.

Growing health consciousness and concerns about the effects of chemicals, drugs, and genetic modifications started to weigh heavily on the public mind at the end of the last century and continued to blossom in the new millennium. The U.S. government began to require detailed nutritional labeling in 1990, allowing consumers to see what was in the food they were buying and thus giving the consumer a larger, more powerful role in purchasing decisions. Presently, finding organic food in every category has become a much easier task in both urban and rural communities.

Those few small organic farms and ranches began to expand as demand slowly increased. Larger companies realized the opportunity and invested in methods to raise more organic products or to acquire more experienced independent providers. What started as a small but determined practice has become mainstream.

For many people, finding delicious and increasingly affordable organic food is becoming easier. The big supermarket chains have allowed all of us to find a range of food. Companies such as Whole Foods and Sprouts continue to lead the expansion of organic produce. They have helped to ignite further acceptance by retailers both large and small, boosting supply to match consumer demand.

The decision every person must make is whether buying organic food, even at a slightly higher price, will make them healthier and happier and even extend their life. Evidence continues to support that living organically is a lifestyle worth everyone's effort. Whether you choose only certain food categories or indulge across the board, it will certainly bring meaningful benefits.

SPRING

Seasonal Produce (March–June)

Apricots

Artichokes

Asparagus

Avocado

Blueberry

Casaba Melon

Cherries

Chives

Collard Greens

Endive

Fava Beans

Fiddlehead Ferns

Lettuce

Limes

Loquats

Mango

Maple Syrup

Mint

Morels

Mustard Greens

Navel Orange

Nectarines

Peaches

Peas

Pineapple

Plums

Pluots

Radishes

Ramps

Rhubarb

Strawberries

Vidalia Onions

Watercress

Recipes

Mango Mousse

1 teaspoon powdered
   gelatin

2 tablespoons water

2 medium mangos, ripe

½ teaspoon fresh lemon
   juice

5 tablespoons sugar

½ cup yogurt (I prefer
   Fage)

This delicious mousse pays homage to Mango Lassi, the popular yogurt drink of India. Use very ripe mangos to get the best flavor. With only five ingredients, the mousse comes together pretty quickly. Just make sure to give the mousse enough time to set up in the refrigerator before serving.

Directions

Sprinkle the gelatin over 1 tablespoon water and set aside to soften.

Use a peeler to remove the mango skins. Cut the fruit into small pieces and place in a blender along with the lemon juice. Purée until smooth.

Add the softened gelatin to a small pot over medium heat along with sugar and another tablespoon of water. Stir until the sugar and gelatin have dissolved. Pour into the blender and pulse to incorporate. Strain the mixture into a large bowl and use a whisk to fold in the yogurt. Pour mousse into 4 individual ramekins, cover with plastic, and let set up in refrigerator for at least 2 hours before serving.

Maple Crème Caramel

MAKES 1 (1½-QUART) DISH (4-6 SERVINGS)

This crème caramel is the perfect dessert to make in early spring during maple syrup season. The maple flavor in this dessert is evident yet not overpowering. I love serving this dessert slightly warmed with some gingersnap cookies.

Directions

Stir together the sugar and 3 tablespoons water in a small pot over high heat. Remove from heat. Continue to boil the mixture until it reaches a dark golden brown. Immediately pour the sugar into a 1½-quart baking dish. Tilt the dish to spread the sugar all over the bottom and set aside.

Preheat the oven to 350°F. Place a baking dish (larger than the dish you are baking the crème caramel in) on the middle rack and fill it 2 inches deep with water.

Add the maple syrup, milk, cream, and salt to a medium pot and bring to a boil over high heat. Remove from heat. Whisk the yolks and egg in a large bowl. Whisk a ladleful of the hot milk mixture into the eggs. Repeat until all the milk is incorporated. Strain the mixture into the prepared baking dish. Cover with foil and poke 5 holes on top to allow steam to escape. Carefully place the dish into the water bath. Bake until the custard is soft and wiggly (look for the Jell-O jiggle), about 1½ hours. Let the crème caramel set up in the refrigerator overnight.

When ready to serve, dip the bottom half of the crème caramel dish in hot water for 15 seconds. Dip a paring knife in the hot water and run it along the inside rim to loosen the sides. Flip out the custard onto a serving dish with raised edges.

½ cup sugar
3 tablespoons water
½ cup maple syrup
1 cup whole milk
1 cup heavy cream
Pinch of salt
4 large egg yolks
1 large egg

Rhubarb Mint Ice Cream

MAKES 4 SERVINGS

2 cups rhubarb, small
diced

1⅓ cups sugar

1 teaspoon water

2 cups whole milk

¼ teaspoon salt

5 mint sprigs

4 large egg yolks

1 cup sour cream

Rhubarb and mint combine to make this delicious and unique ice cream. The earthy mint hits you first, followed by the sweet rhubarb. The delicious tang of sour cream comes across your palette at the end, perfectly tying all the flavors together.

Directions

Add the rhubarb, ⅓ cup sugar, and 1 teaspoon water to a pot and cook over medium heat until softened, about 6 to 8 minutes. Transfer rhubarb to a clean bowl and set aside to cool.

In the same pot, bring the milk, remaining sugar, and salt to just a boil over high heat. Remove from heat, add the mint sprigs, cover, and let steep for 10 minutes.

Remove the mint and re-warm the milk over medium heat. Place the yolks in a large bowl and slowly whisk in a cup of the hot milk. Return the yolk mixture to the pot and whisk in well. Continue stirring over medium heat until the mixture begins to thicken. Remove from heat and whisk in the sour cream. Strain the mixture into a clean container, stir in the cooked rhubarb, and place uncovered in the refrigerator until completely cool. Churn in an ice cream maker and store in freezer.

Rhubarb Cardamom Cake

MAKES 1 (9X5X3-INCH) LOAF

The texture and shape of this cake is similar to a pound cake, but what makes it so much more is the gorgeous red sweet-tart rhubarb on top and the hidden layers of soft rhubarb in the middle. This cake is lightly flavored with cardamom, ginger, and orange liquor. April is the perfect month to make this stunning cake.

Directions

Preheat oven to 350°F. Place a baking sheet on the middle rack (you will bake the cake on this tray). Grease a 9x5x3-inch loaf pan and line the bottom and sides with parchment paper. Set aside.

Warm the milk, cardamom pods, and ginger in a small pot over medium heat. Remove from heat, cover, and let steep for 10 minutes. While the mixture steeps, cut the rhubarb stalks into 3-inch long pieces. Working with one piece at a time, stand the cut-side down on a cutting board and carefully slice ⅛-inch thick strips. Lay the strips on a plate and set aside.

In a mixer fitted with the paddle attachment, cream the sugar, butter, Cointreau, and vanilla on medium speed until light and fluffy, about 2 minutes. Scrape bowl well. Add the eggs one at a time, mixing well after each addition. Scrape bowl well. Add the flour, baking powder, and salt. Strain the steeped milk over the dry ingredients in the mixing bowl. Mix on low speed for 30 seconds. Scrape bowl well. Mix on medium speed for 10 seconds.

Transfer ⅓ of the batter to the prepared pan. Arrange a single layer of rhubarb on top and cover with another ⅓ of the batter. Arrange a layer of rhubarb on top and cover with remaining batter. Lay a final layer of rhubarb on top and sprinkle with a little sugar. Place loaf on the sheet tray and bake for 60 minutes. Some batter may overflow onto the sheet tray during baking. After 60 minutes, cover the loaf with a loose tent of foil and bake for 20 minutes more or until an inserted toothpick comes out clean.

½ cup whole milk

8 cardamom pods, crushed

1-inch piece of ginger, peeled and thinly sliced

2–3 rhubarb stalks

1¼ cups sugar

1 cup unsalted butter, soft

1 tablespoon Cointreau or orange liqueur

1 teaspoon vanilla extract

4 large eggs

2 cups all-purpose flour

1½ teaspoons baking powder

1 teaspoon salt

Sugar for sprinkling

Peach Dumplings

MAKES 4 SERVINGS

1 roll of phyllo dough,
  thawed
1 cup plus 4 teaspoons
  unsalted butter, soft
Sugar for sprinkling
2 large ripe peaches,
  halved and pitted
4 teaspoons brown sugar

I love peaches. Lucky for me peach season begins in spring and extends through summer and into early autumn, giving me ample time to indulge in making a smorgasbord of peach desserts. These peach dumplings are made with flaky phyllo dough, which gives them a crispy exterior that encases a warm, juicy peach. Your guests will be blown away by the delicious sweetness of fresh peach in every bite of this lovely dessert.

Directions

Preheat oven to 375°F. Line a sheet tray with parchment paper and set aside.

Unroll the thawed phyllo dough on the counter and separate the top sheet. Keep the remaining sheets covered with a damp paper towel. Melt 1 cup of butter in the microwave. Use a pastry brush to butter the sheet and generously sprinkle with some sugar (1 to 2 teaspoons). Repeat this step with two more phyllo sheets. Lay a fourth sheet perpendicular to the other sheets and brush again with butter and sprinkle with sugar. Place a peach half in the middle and fill the fruit's center with a teaspoon of brown sugar and a teaspoon of butter. Bring up the sides of dough and gather it at the top, twisting it slightly to tighten. Brush the dumpling with butter, sprinkle with some sugar, and place on prepared sheet tray. Repeat this step with the other peach halves.

Bake for 15 minutes, rotate tray, and bake 15 minutes more until golden brown. Let rest for 5 minutes before serving.

Peach Cobbler

MAKES 1 (1½-QUART) COBBLER

(ABOUT 6 SERVINGS)

This is one of the first desserts I like to make when peaches come into season. It's easy to make and doesn't require many ingredients or steps. The buttery cobbler topping has a tender, cake-like texture which blends well with the soft, juicy peaches below.

Directions

Preheat oven to 375°F. Use a peeler to remove the peach skins. Cut the peaches in half, remove the pits, and slice each half into 4 wedges. Place wedges into a large bowl and toss with 4 tablespoons sugar and lemon juice. Transfer fruit to a 1½-quart baking dish. Set aside.

In a mixer fitted with the paddle attachment, cream the butter and remaining sugar on medium speed until light and fluffy, about 2 minutes. Add the egg and mix for another minute. Scrape bowl well. Add the flour, baking powder, and salt and mix just until incorporated. Drop spoonfuls of the dough on top of the peaches. Bake until top is golden brown, about 45 to 55 minutes.

5 large peaches, ripe

4 tablespoons sugar plus ⅓ cup sugar

1 tablespoon fresh lemon juice

3 ounces unsalted butter, soft

1 large egg

⅔ cup all-purpose flour

¼ teaspoon baking powder

Pinch salt

Navel Orange Rosemary Sorbet

MAKES 4 SERVINGS

2 cups fresh navel orange
juice

1 cup strawberries, hulled
and halved

½ cup sugar

1 tablespoon chopped
rosemary

¼ teaspoon salt

This lovely sorbet is best made in springtime when navel oranges are at their peak. I add some fresh strawberries to bring body, sweetness, and hue to this delightful sorbet. The rosemary adds a nice herbal flavor that complements citrus well.

Directions

Combine all the ingredients in a blender and mix on high speed until mixture is smooth, about 30 seconds. Push mixture through a mesh strainer. Discard pulp. Chill sorbet base in the refrigerator for 1 hour. Churn in an ice cream maker. Let set up in the freezer if you prefer a firmer consistency.

Cherry Ice Cream Sandwiches

MAKES 8 SANDWICHES

Ice Cream Base
(made the day before):

24 ounces whole milk

12 ounces heavy cream

4 ounces sugar

12 large egg yolks

½ tablespoon vanilla
  extract

1 teaspoon almond
  extract

Roasted Cherries
(made the day before):

1 pound cherries, pitted
  and halved

2 tablespoons sugar

1 tablespoon rum or
  kirsch

Chocolate Cookie
(made the day before):

½ cup unsalted butter,
  soft

½ cup sugar

1 large egg

½ cup all-purpose flour

¼ cup unsweetened
  cocoa powder

½ teaspoon baking
  powder

These cherry ice cream sandwiches are always a showstopper. I roast the cherries first to release their juices, ensuring that the resulting ice cream is super flavorful. All the components need to be made the day before, so plan ahead. Cherries have a distinct season that begins in early June and lasts through August. By September they are virtually gone from the markets, so make sure to get your cherry fill within those months.

Make cherry ice cream:
Bring the milk, heavy cream, and half the sugar to a boil over high heat. Whisk the remaining sugar and yolks in a large bowl. Slowly whisk in half of the hot milk mixture to the bowl, one cup at a time. Pour egg mixture into the pot and cook over medium heat until liquid thickens, stirring constantly (do not boil). Strain mixture into a large container. Stir in the extracts. Press down a layer of plastic wrap on top of the surface and keep in refrigerator to cool overnight.

Make roasted cherries:
Preheat oven to 400°F. Toss the cherries, sugar, and rum in a large bowl. Transfer to a baking pan and roast in the oven for 30 to 45 minutes until thick and bubbly, stirring every 15 minutes. Let sit on counter to cool.

Make chocolate cookie:
Preheat the oven to 350°F. Grease a 13x18-inch rimmed baking sheet and line the bottom with parchment paper, leaving a 2-inch overhang on the two shorter sides.

In a mixer fitted with the paddle attachment, mix the butter and sugar on medium speed until light and fluffy, about 1 minute. Beat in the egg. Add the flour, cocoa powder, and baking powder. Mix until incorporated, about 1 minute more. Make sure to scrape the bowl to ensure ingredients are fully combined.

Using a mini offset spatula, spread the batter evenly in the prepared pan. Make sure to smooth the top. Bake for 8 minutes. Remove from oven and let cool completely.

The next day:

Gently remove the chocolate cookie from the pan and invert it onto a cutting board. Remove the parchment, cut the cake in half, and place one of the halves on a large piece of foil.

Remove the ice cream base from the refrigerator, fold in the roasted cherries, and churn in an ice cream maker. Using a mini offset spatula, spread the ice cream over the cake half that is on the foil. Slide the other cake half off the cutting board and onto the ice cream. Press down gently. Wrap the foil up and around the assembled dessert. Place in the freezer at least 4 hours.

When ice cream is fully set, remove the dessert from the freezer and trim the edges if necessary. Cut the rectangle into 8 pieces. Individually wrap each ice cream sandwich with parchment paper, wax paper, or aluminum foil and tape to seal. Store the sandwiches in an airtight container in the freezer for up to a week.

Stone Fruit Tarts

MAKES 3 TARTS

These gorgeous tarts showcase the stone fruits of spring: apricots, plums, and cherries. Using store-bought puff pastry makes creating these a breeze. These tarts are best eaten the day they're made.

Directions

Preheat oven to 400°F. Remove puff pastry sheet from freezer and let thaw at room temperature. Line a sheet tray with parchment paper and set aside.

Place each of the three fruits in a separate bowl and add 1 tablespoon of agave to each bowl. Toss the fruit well and set aside.

When the puff pastry has thawed, roll the sheet out to ⅛-inch thickness on a lightly floured surface, doing your best to maintain its rectangular shape. Cut the sheet into three equal strips with a sharp knife. Place each strip on the prepared sheet tray.

Brush the tops of the puff pastry with the egg white. Arrange the fruit on top, leaving a ½-inch border. Sprinkle the fruit and edges with sparkling sugar. Bake 20 to 25 minutes until tarts are golden brown.

1 frozen puff pastry sheet (I recommend Pepperidge Farm)

3 apricots, pitted and thinly sliced

2 plums or pluots, pitted and thinly sliced

1 cup cherries, pitted and halved

3 tablespoons agave nectar

1 large egg white, whisked

Sparkling sugar for sprinkling

Grilled Peaches and Cream Cake

MAKES 1 (9-INCH) TRIPLE LAYER CAKE

3¼ cups cake flour

4½ teaspoons baking powder

1½ teaspoons salt

2¼ cups plus 3 tablespoons sugar

1¼ cups unsalted butter, soft

3 teaspoons vanilla extract

1½ cups whole milk, slightly warmed

8 large egg whites

2 cups raspberries

3–4 large ripe peaches, pitted and halved

3 tablespoons olive oil

½ cup sliced almonds

2 cups heavy cream, chilled

In this stunning dessert, layers of raspberry white cake are stacked between clouds of sweetened whipped cream. The cake is finished with grilled peach slices, fresh raspberries, and toasted almonds. Any variety of peach works well in this cake.

Directions

Preheat oven to 375°F. Line three 9-inch round cake pans with parchment paper and grease well with pan spray. Set aside.

Sift the flour, baking powder, and salt. Set aside.

In a mixer fitted with the paddle attachment, cream the 2¼ cups sugar, butter, and 2 teaspoons vanilla on medium speed until light and fluffy, about 2 minutes. Scrape bowl well. Alternately add the dry ingredients and milk in three portions, mixing well after each addition.

In a separate bowl, whisk the egg whites to medium-stiff peaks. Gently fold the whites into the cake batter in three equal portions. Fold in 1 cup of raspberries along with the last portion of whites. Evenly distribute the cake batter into the three prepared pans and bake for 20 minutes or until an inserted toothpick comes out clean. Let cakes cool completely.

Turn on your grill to high heat. Slice some of the peach halves into quarters and toss all the peaches with the olive oil in a large bowl. Place the peaches on the grill and cook until fruit is cooked through and has grill marks, about 4 minutes per side. Return finished peaches to bowl. Set aside.

Place the almonds in a small sauté pan over medium heat. Shake the pan continuously and toast the almonds until golden brown, about 5 minutes. Set aside.

In a mixer fitted with the whip attachment, beat the heavy cream and remaining sugar and vanilla on high speed until medium peaks form.

Slice off tops of cake. Spread the whipped cream between the cake layers and top with the grilled peaches, remaining raspberries, and toasted almonds.

White Peach and Cherry Crumble

MAKES 1 (1½-QUART) CRUMBLE

(ABOUT 4 SERVINGS)

When the long days of spring are in full swing, bright red cherries and gorgeous white peaches flood the market. Though delicious on their own, they pair remarkably well in this springtime crumble. The addition of sweet wine adds a noticeable richness to the filling and the double layer of brown sugar oat crumb ensures that every spoonful has a crunchy bite. If you're not a wine lover, simply substitute it with water and increase the sugar a bit.

Make crumble:

Preheat oven to 350°F. Butter a 1½-quart baking dish with 1 tablespoon of butter. Set aside.

Melt the remaining butter and place in a medium bowl. Add the flour, brown sugar, oats, almonds, and cinnamon. Mix well with your hands. Transfer ⅓ of the mixture to the prepared dish and pat down.

Make filling:

Combine the cherries, peach, lemon zest, and vanilla in a bowl and toss to coat. Transfer to the prepared dish over the layer of crumble.

Combine the sweet wine, sugar, and cornstarch in a small pot over medium heat. Bring to a boil for 1 minute, stirring constantly. Pour sauce over the fruit mixture. Top with the remaining oat mixture. Bake for 30 minutes until filling bubbles.

Crumble:

5 tablespoons unsalted butter, soft

½ cup all-purpose flour

½ cup brown sugar

⅓ cup oats

¼ cup sliced almonds

¼ teaspoon cinnamon

Filling:

2 cups cherries, pitted and halved

1 white peach, pitted and cut into bite-size pieces

1 teaspoon lemon zest

1 teaspoon vanilla extract

½ cup sweet wine (I recommend Tokaji)

¼ cup sugar

1 tablespoon cornstarch

Apricot Peach Crostata
MAKES 1 (9½-INCH) TART

Apricot Peach Jam:

2 cups apricots, pitted
   and medium diced

2 cups peaches, pitted
   and medium diced

2 tablespoons lemon
   juice

¾ cup sugar

½ teaspoon nutmeg

½ teaspoon vanilla
   extract

1 cinnamon stick

Pinch of salt

Crust:

1½ cups all-purpose flour

1 tablespoon sugar

¼ teaspoon salt

½ cup unsalted butter,
   cold and cubed

1 large egg, separated

1 tablespoon water

Sugar for sprinkling

Apricot and peach pair wondrously in this beautiful crostata. Cinnamon, nutmeg, and vanilla flavor the jam as it cooks down to a thick, spreadable consistency. The intense and robust jam is spread onto the buttery, cookie-like crust and topped with a beautiful lattice design.

Make the jam:

Combine all the jam ingredients in a large pot and bring to a low boil over medium heat. Cook until thickened, about 25 minutes, stirring occasionally. Remove cinnamon stick, transfer to a clean bowl, and set aside to cool.

Make the crust:

Preheat oven to 400°F. Combine the flour, sugar, and salt in a mixer fitted with the paddle attachment. Add the butter and mix until it breaks down to pea size. Whisk the egg yolk and 1 tablespoon water. Add to the dry ingredients and mix until dough comes together. Form into a disc, wrap with plastic, and chill in refrigerator for 20 minutes.

Roll out ⅔ of the dough into a circle of ¼-inch thickness on a floured surface. Carefully line the tart pan with the dough and poke holes on the bottom with a fork. Chill the tart shell in the refrigerator for 10 minutes. Roll out the remaining dough and scraps to ⅛-inch thickness and cut ten (½-inch) wide strips. Spread the jam onto the tart crust. Lay the strips in a lattice fashion on top of the jam. Brush the strips with the whisked egg white and sprinkle some sugar on top. Bake for 10 minutes. Reduce heat to 375°F. Bake 20 minutes more. Let cool completely before slicing.

Roasted Apricot Sherbet

MAKES 4 SERVINGS

Roasting is an easy way to bring out the wonderful flavor of apricot that we all know exists but is sometimes hard to detect when apricots are eaten fresh. This smooth sherbet is highly addictive and soars with the lively flavor of apricot and the creaminess of gelato.

Directions

Preheat oven to 400°F. Coat a 9x13-inch baking dish with the butter. Place the apricots in the dish cut side up. Sprinkle the fruit with 1 tablespoon of sugar. Bake for 20 to 25 minutes until apricots are fragrant and tender. Set aside.

Bring ½ cup sugar and ¼ cup water to a boil in a small pot over high heat. Pour into a blender and top with the roasted apricots and salt. Purée until smooth. Transfer to a clean container and let chill overnight in the refrigerator.

The next day, stir in the cream and churn in an ice cream maker. Serve immediately or keep in freezer if you prefer a firmer sherbet.

1 tablespoon unsalted butter, soft
1 pound ripe apricots, halved and pitted
1 tablespoon plus ½ cup sugar
¼ cup water
¼ teaspoon salt
1 cup heavy cream

Strawberry Rhubarb Pie

MAKES 1 (9½-INCH) PIE

When April rolls around, you'll start seeing long crimson stalks of rhubarb at the markets. Choose ones that are firm and free of blemishes, and please remember that the leaves are toxic. Rhubarb itself is very tart, but when combined with sweet strawberries, as in this pie, it becomes absolutely divine.

Crust:

2 ½ cups all-purpose flour

1 teaspoon sugar

1 teaspoon salt

1 cup unsalted butter, cold and cubed

⅓ cup plus 1 tablespoon ice water

Filling:

1 pound rhubarb, cut into ½-inch thick slices

1 pound strawberries, hulled and quartered

¾ cup sugar

¼ cup cornstarch

1 teaspoon lemon zest

1 teaspoon lemon juice

2 tablespoons unsalted butter, soft

1 large egg white

1 teaspoon water

1 teaspoon sugar

Make crust:

Combine flour, sugar, and salt in mixer fitted with the paddle attachment and blend on low speed to incorporate. Add the cubed butter and mix on low speed until butter is broken down to pea size. Add the ice water all at once and mix just until dough comes together. Separate dough into two equal pieces and shape them into flat discs. Roll out each piece on a lightly floured surface to about ⅛-inch thickness. Place one disc on a flat plate and keep in the refrigerator for later. Line the pie dish with the remaining disc. Trim the dough flush with the pie dish and place in refrigerator to chill.

Make filling:

Preheat oven to 400°F. Combine the rhubarb, strawberries, sugar, cornstarch, lemon zest, and juice in a large bowl and toss well. Add to the prepared pie dish and dot filling with 2 tablespoons of butter. Whisk the egg white with 1 teaspoon water. Brush the rim of the bottom crust with the egg wash and lay the top crust from the refrigerator over the filling. Pinch and flute the edges to seal. Brush a thin layer of egg wash over the top and sprinkle with some sugar. Use a sharp paring knife to cut vents in top crust. Bake for 20 minutes. Reduce oven temperature to 350°F and bake for 35 to 45 minutes more until filling bubbles and crust is golden brown.

Nectarine Tart

MAKES 1 (9½-INCH) TART

Nectarines arrive in May and stay throughout the summer months. In California, the nectarines found during the tail end of the season are especially delicious and perfect for making this beautiful tart. Sweet nectarines and a crunchy graham crust combine with a luscious blend of cream cheese and mascarpone to create a fragrant cheesecake-like tart.

Make crust:

Preheat oven to 350°F. Grease the tart pan. Combine the graham crumbs and sugar in a medium bowl. Mix in the melted butter with your hands. Press mixture evenly against the bottom and sides of the prepared tart pan. Bake for 10 minutes. Place in refrigerator to cool.

Make filling:

In a mixer fitted with the paddle attachment, mix the cream cheese and mascarpone on low speed for 1 minute until smooth. Add the sugar, lemon zest, and vanilla and continue mixing until incorporated. Blend in the milk. Transfer to the cooled tart shell and spread smoothly with a mini offset spatula. Place in refrigerator for at least 2 hours to set up.

Halve, pit, and cut the nectarines into thin slices. Toss them in a large bowl with the olive oil and lemon juice. Arrange the slices in a concentric pattern on top of the filling. Tart is best served the day it's made.

Crust:

1½ cups graham crumbs

¼ cup sugar

½ cup unsalted butter, melted

Filling:

8 ounces cream cheese, room temperature

8 ounces mascarpone

½ cup sugar

1 teaspoon lemon zest

1 teaspoon vanilla extract

2 tablespoons whole milk

3–4 ripe nectarines

1 tablespoon fruity olive oil

½ teaspoon lemon juice

Fruitcake 2.0

MAKES 1 (10-INCH) TUBE PAN

Fruit:

1 cup rum (I prefer
    Appleton)

¼ cup dried cranberries

¼ cup currants or raisins

8 ounces cherries, pitted
    and halved

2 small apricots, pitted
    and chopped into bite-
    size pieces

1 cup sliced almonds

2 tablespoons sugar

2 teaspoons vanilla extract

1 teaspoon almond extract

Cake:

12 tablespoons unsalted
    butter, soft

½ cup brown sugar

½ cup sugar

2 large eggs

1½ cups all-purpose flour

1 teaspoon baking powder

¼ teaspoon cinnamon

Fruitcake 2.0 is my updated version of the popular holiday "favorite." I have developed a recipe that uses a mix of fresh and dried fruits and doesn't require multiple days to make. My farm-to-table version has sweet cherries, fresh apricots, and a handful of almonds, currants, and cranberries. Rum is my alcohol of choice for this cake, but I have a feeling bourbon whiskey would be a great choice, too.

Directions

Preheat oven to 300°F. Grease a 10-inch tube pan and set aside.

Warm the rum in a small pot over medium heat. Place the cranberries and currants in a small bowl and pour the rum over the fruit to rehydrate them. Set aside.

Combine the cherries, apricots, almonds, sugar, and extracts in a large bowl and toss well. Set aside.

In a mixer fitted with the paddle attachment, cream the butter and sugars on medium speed until light and fluffy, about 2 minutes. Add the eggs one at a time on low speed and scrape well after each addition. Add the flour, baking powder, and cinnamon and mix just until incorporated. Drain and reserve the rum from the cranberry-currant mixture and add the fruit to the mixing bowl along with the cherry mixture. Mix until the fruits are evenly distributed. Scrape bowl well and transfer batter to prepared pan.

Bake for 45 minutes or until an inserted toothpick comes out clean. While cake bakes, reduce the rum in a small pot over high heat until about ¼ cup remains. Poke about 20 holes on top of the baked cake and pour the reduced rum on top. Let cool completely before removing cake from pan.

SUMMER

Seasonal Produce (June-September)

Apricots
Artichokes
Avocado
Cherries
Beets
Bell Peppers
Black Currants
Blackberries
Blueberries
Boysenberries
Lettuce
Cantaloupe
Casaba Melon
Champagne Grapes
Chayote Squash
Cherries
Corn
Cucumbers
Durian
Eggplant

Figs
Grapes
Green Beans
Guava
Honeydew
Huckleberries
Jackfruit
Jalapeño Peppers
Key Limes
Lavender
Lima Beans
Limes
Loganberries
Lychee
Mango
Mulberries
Nectarines
Okra
Papaya
Passion Fruit

Peaches
Peas
Pineapple
Plums
Pluots
Potatoes
Radishes
Ramps
Raspberries
Rhubarb
Shallots
Soybeans
Strawberries
Sugar Apple
Sugar Snap Peas
Summer Squash
Tomatoes
Watermelon
Zucchini

Recipes

Strawberry Hand Pies

MAKES ABOUT 10 HAND PIES

These cute hand pies are perfect for those summer days when strawberries are at their peak. Roasting the strawberries with vanilla bean intensifies their flavor and removes their water content. As a result, you are left with an intensely flavored pie without that annoying gap between the top crust and the filling below. These pies can be made ahead of time, individually frozen, and baked off later when desired.

Directions

Preheat oven to 375°F. Cut the strawberries into small pieces (I like to cut them into quarters) and place them in a medium bowl. Sift the powdered sugar onto the strawberries. Scrape the vanilla bean and add to the bowl along with the pod. Toss the berries well until no trace of powdered sugar remains. Transfer to a 9-inch pie plate or cake pan. Roast in oven for 15 minutes. Use a fork to break up the fruit. Roast 15 minutes more. Use a fork to break up any chunks of fruit that remain. Place in refrigerator to cool while you make the dough.

In a large mixing bowl with the paddle attachment, add the flours, sugar, and salt. Mix on low speed and slowly add the cubed butter. Increase speed to medium and continue mixing until butter breaks down to pea size. Whisk the water and egg yolk in a small bowl and add all at once to the mixer. Mix on low speed just until dough comes together. Form dough into a disc and wrap in plastic. Let chill in refrigerator for 15 minutes.

Line a sheet tray with parchment paper and set aside. On a lightly floured surface, roll out the chilled dough to ¼-inch thickness. Use a 4-inch round cutter to portion out 5 circles and place them on the prepared tray with space between. Whisk the egg white and brush a thin layer onto each round. Spoon a small mound of the roasted strawberries in the center of each round leaving a ½-inch border. Cut out 5 more rounds of dough and place on top of the strawberries. Gently press down along the edges to seal well. Use a fork to crimp the edges. Poke holes on top with the fork. Brush with egg white and sprinkle with some sparkling sugar. Place pies in freezer for 10 minutes to set up.

Bake for 20 to 22 minutes, until pies are lightly browned. Let cool slightly before serving.

Filling:
1 pint strawberries, washed and hulled
¼ cup powdered sugar
½ of a vanilla bean, split lengthwise

Dough:
1½ cups all-purpose flour
½ cup whole wheat flour
1½ tablespoons sugar
1 teaspoon salt
1 cup unsalted butter, cold and cubed
2 tablespoons ice water
1 large egg, separated
Sparkling sugar for sprinkling

Casaba Melon
with Sweet Wine Gelée

MAKES 4-5 SERVINGS

1 cup sweet wine
   (I like Tokaji)
2 teaspoons powdered
   gelatin
1 tablespoon sugar
1 large casaba melon, ripe
1 lemon

The first time I tried casaba melon I was blown away by its subtle sweet taste. Imagine watering down a honeydew with a cucumber and that's the wonderful flavor of this melon. Its delicate taste and soft juicy flesh make it satisfying enough to serve as is, but I prefer to dress it up by pairing it with a potent sweet wine gelée and some fresh lemon zest.

Directions

Line the bottom and sides of a 6- or 8-inch square pan with plastic wrap and set aside.

In a small bowl, stir 2 tablespoons of wine with the powdered gelatin and set aside. In a small pot, warm the remaining wine with the sugar and stir until sugar is dissolved. Remove from heat, stir in the gelatin, and pour into the prepared pan. Place in refrigerator until set, about 1 hour.

Slice the melon in half and remove the seeds. Use a melon baller to scoop out the flesh and arrange the balls on plates.

After the gelée is fully set, flip it out onto a cutting board. Carefully remove the plastic and cut the gelée into small pieces. Arrange pieces around the melon balls. Garnish with lemon zest.

Sweet Corn Panna Cotta with Blackberries

MAKES 4 SERVINGS

In California, ears of corn start popping up in July. Panna cotta is a beautiful dessert that exquisitely showcases this summer vegetable. The sugar from the corn infuses with the cream while the starch helps make the panna cotta silky smooth. The blackberry component provides a sweet-tart flavor to balance everything out.

Make panna cotta:

Slice kernels from corn and place in a large bowl. Break the ears in half with your hands and add to the bowl. Set aside.

In a small bowl, combine 2 tablespoons of half and half with the gelatin and stir until combined. Set aside.

Combine the remaining half and half, sugar, and salt in a large pot over high heat and bring to a bowl. Remove from heat and carefully add the corn ears and kernels to the pot. Cover and let steep for 20 minutes.

Strain the corn from the cream mixture and stir in the gelatin. (Don't throw away the kernels! Sauté them with a little butter and enjoy them as a side dish.) Pour into desired vessels. Let set up in refrigerator for at least 2 hours.

Make blackberry sauce:

In a small pot, combine the blackberries, water, and sugar. Bring to a boil over medium heat and cook for 5 minutes, stirring occasionally. Remove from heat and let cool on the counter while panna cotta continues to set up in refrigerator.

When panna cotta is set, invert panna cotta onto serving plates and top with the blackberry sauce.

Corn Panna Cotta:

2 large ears of sweet corn

2 cups half and half

1½ teaspoons powdered gelatin

3 tablespoons sugar

¼ teaspoon salt

Blackberry Sauce:

1 cup blackberries

¼ cup water

1 tablespoon sugar

Blueberry Crisp
MAKES A 1-QUART CRISP

Filling:

1 tablespoon unsalted
    butter, soft

12 ounces blueberries

⅓ cup sugar

1 tablespoon all-purpose
    flour

½ teaspoon cinnamon

Crisp:

¾ cup all-purpose flour

¼ cup brown sugar

½ teaspoon salt

¼ cup unsalted butter,
    melted

1 tablespoon sugar

This blueberry crisp is delightfully delicious and easy to pull together. The topping is a simple mixture of flour, sugar, and butter that remains crisp well after being baked; a perfect contrast to the soft, juicy berries below.

Directions

Preheat oven to 350°F. Coat the bottom of a 1-quart baking dish with 1 tablespoon butter and set aside.

In a large bowl, toss the blueberries, sugar, flour, and cinnamon together. Transfer to the prepared dish.

In the same bowl, mix the flour, brown sugar, and salt. Add the melted butter and mix with your hands until mixture resembles loose sand. Sprinkle the topping evenly over the fruit. Sprinkle a tablespoon of sugar on top. Bake for 40 to 45 minutes until filling bubbles and crisp is golden brown.

Summer Squash Cake
MAKES 1 (9- OR 10-INCH) ROUND CAKE

Summer squash is harvested while immature when its rind and seeds are still tender and edible. This cake is packed with summer squash, making it both super moist and healthy. Topped with a luscious cream cheese frosting, this vegetable-based cake is one of the most mouth-watering desserts in the book.

Make the cake:
Preheat oven to 350°F. Grease a 9- or 10-inch round pan and set aside.

In a large bowl, whisk the eggs, squash, sugar, oil, and vanilla extract well. Add the remaining ingredients and mix until incorporated. Transfer to prepared pan and bake for 55 to 60 minutes, or until inserted toothpick comes out clean. Cool completely.

Make the cream cheese frosting:
Sift the powdered sugar and set aside. In a mixer fitted with the paddle attachment, beat the cream cheese, butter, and vanilla on medium speed until well blended. Scrape down the sides of the bowl and mix for 30 seconds to ensure no lumps remain. Add the powdered sugar all at once and mix on low speed until sugar is just incorporated. Scrape bowl well and beat on high speed for 10 seconds.

Remove cooled cake from pan and place onto a serving platter. Cut the rounded cake top off, if desired. Spread cream cheese frosting on top in a decorative design. Store cake in refrigerator.

Cake:
3 large eggs
2 cups grated summer squash
1½ cups sugar
1 cup vegetable oil
1 teaspoon vanilla extract
2 cups all-purpose flour
1 teaspoon cinnamon
1 teaspoon baking powder
½ teaspoon baking soda
¼ teaspoon salt

Cream Cheese Frosting:
3½ cups powdered sugar
1 (8-ounce) package cream cheese, room temperature
¼ cup unsalted butter, room temperature
1 teaspoon vanilla extract

Guava Cheesecake

MAKES 1 (9-INCH) CHEESECAKE

8 large guavas, very ripe

1 cup sugar

Pinch of salt

2 cups graham crackers, crushed

½ cup unsalted butter, melted

2 (8-ounce) packages cream cheese, room temperature

3 large eggs

1 cup sugar

1 pint sour cream

1 teaspoon vanilla extract

I will always remember the first time I tried guava. It was in northeast India and I was ten years old. I couldn't help but notice these peculiar green fruits hanging in the trees above, scattered on the lawns below and smooshed all over the streets; they were everywhere! My cousin pulled one off a tree and said, "Eat it!" And so, I ate it. It was love at first bite. The flesh was a gorgeous light pink and had a distinct pear-strawberry flavor that I had never tasted before. I don't see guavas too much in California, but when I do I grab them up as quickly as possible. While delicious eaten fresh, guavas also pair beautifully with cream cheese. Make sure to use very ripe guavas in this recipe to achieve the most flavorful purée.

Directions

Peel and halve the guavas. Scoop out the seeds and discard them. Place the guava halves in a large pan and cover with water. Cook uncovered over medium heat until soft, about 15 minutes. Remove from heat and strain out the water. Sprinkle 1 cup sugar over the guava and use a potato masher to break up the fruit. Return pan to the heat and cook at a rolling boil for 10 minutes, stirring occasionally. The mixture will start to thicken and the liquid will cook off. Continue cooking until mixture resembles applesauce. Remove from heat and stir in a pinch of salt. Push the mixture through a mesh strainer and discard pulp. Let guava purée cool in the refrigerator while you make the cheesecake crust and batter.

Preheat oven to 325°F. Grease a 9-inch cake pan. Place a large baking dish on the middle rack and fill it 1-inch deep with water. You will bake the cheesecake in the water bath.

Combine the crushed grahams and butter in a large bowl and mix well with your hands. Press the mixture into the bottom and 1-inch up the sides of the prepared pan. Set aside.

In a mixer fitted with the paddle attachment, beat the cream cheese until smooth. Add the eggs one at a time, scraping the bowl well after each addition. Stir in the sugar and mix until well blended. Stir in the sour cream and vanilla. Transfer batter to the prepared pan. Drop spoonfuls of the guava purée onto the batter and use a toothpick to create a swirled pattern. Bake the cheesecake in the water bath until the center is set and has a slight Jell-O jiggle, about 60 to 75 minutes. Remove from oven and place cheesecake in the refrigerator to set up for at least 6 hours or overnight.

When cake is completely cool, run a sharp paring knife around the edges and unmold the cheesecake onto a serving plate.

Raspberry Martini
MAKES 2 MARTINIS

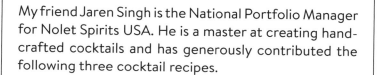

My friend Jaren Singh is the National Portfolio Manager for Nolet Spirits USA. He is a master at creating hand-crafted cocktails and has generously contributed the following three cocktail recipes.

6–8 raspberries
3 ounces Nolet's Silver
    Dry Gin
2 ounces fresh Meyer
    lemon juice
1 ounce simple syrup or
    1½ teaspoons agave
Sugar for rims
2 Meyer lemon peels

By combining fresh raspberries and Meyer lemon juice, you can create the perfect dessert martini to sip on as a warm spring day comes to a close. Simple syrup is made with equal parts sugar and water brought to a boil and cooled. If you don't have simple syrup on hand, agave nectar is a fine substitute.

Directions
Add the raspberries, gin, Meyer lemon juice, and syrup to a shaker and top with ice. Vigorously shake and strain into two chilled Martini glasses rimmed with sugar. Garnish each with a lemon peel.

Cucumber Mint Limeade

MAKES 2 LIMEADES

2 Persian cucumbers

12–16 mint leaves, plus
   sprigs for garnish

2 ounces (about 2 limes)
   fresh lime juice

2 ounces simple syrup or
   1 tablespoon agave

3 ounces Ketel One
   Citroen Vodka

Club soda to top

This is a great any-day-any-season cocktail with a clean, light flavor. The cucumber, mint, and lime combine perfectly to create a refreshing beverage that's especially welcoming after a rich, spicy meal.

Directions

Cut 4 to 6 thin cucumber coins and set them aside to use as garnish later. Peel the remaining cucumbers and cut them into coins. Divide them between each drinking glass. Add 6 to 8 mint leaves into each glass and muddle the mint and cucumber. Add the lime juice, syrup, and Ketel One Citroen Vodka. Top with ice and club soda and stir to combine. Garnish with the cucumber coins and a large mint sprig.

Watermelon Sparkler

MAKES 2 SPARKLERS

Watermelon, lime, and gin pair exquisitely in this summertime sparkler. Nolet's Silver Dry Gin is a small batch gin with flavors of Turkish rose, peach, and raspberry, making it the perfect gin to use in a farm-to-table dessert cocktail.

Directions

Slice the watermelon in half. Cut up 2 cups of flesh and set aside 2 small spears for garnish. Muddle the cubed watermelon in a shaker. Add the gin, lime juice, and syrup. Top with ice. Vigorously shake and strain into two chilled flutes. Top with sparkling wine and garnish with the watermelon spears.

1 personal watermelon
3 ounces Nolet's Silver Dry Gin
2 ounces fresh lime juice
1½ ounces simple syrup or 2 teaspoons agave
4 ounces sparkling wine

Huckleberry Panna Cotta

MAKES 4-5 SERVINGS

Streusel Crunch:

6 tablespoons all-
purpose flour

2½ tablespoons brown
sugar

2½ tablespoons sugar

1 teaspoon lemon zest

¼ teaspoon cinnamon

⅛ teaspoon nutmeg

⅛ teaspoon salt

2 tablespoons unsalted
butter, soft

1 teaspoon lemon juice

Panna Cotta:

1¼ teaspoons powdered
gelatin

2 tablespoons whole milk

1½ cups heavy cream

1 cup powdered sugar,
sifted

1 teaspoon vanilla extract

¼ teaspoon salt

¾ cup sour cream

The peak season for finding juicy, delicious huckleberries is late summer and early autumn. Areas of the Pacific Northwest and the mountains of Montana and Idaho are prime picking areas. If you don't live in those regions, it's perfectly fine to use frozen as you can be assured they were picked at their peak.

Make streusel crunch:
Combine the flour, sugars, zest, cinnamon, nutmeg, and salt in a mixer fitted with the paddle attachment. Mix on low speed until incorporated. Add the butter and lemon juice and mix until crumbly. Transfer to a container and store in the freezer.

Make panna cotta:
Whisk together gelatin and milk in a small bowl and set aside. Place 1 cup of cream, sugar, vanilla, and salt in a medium pot. Warm the mixture over medium heat, whisking occasionally until sugar dissolves. Whisk in the gelatin mixture and stir until gelatin dissolves. Strain into a clean bowl and place over an ice bath to cool.

Meanwhile, beat the remaining ½ cup cream to stiff peaks in a mixer fitted with the whip attachment. Whisk in the sour cream. Fold the whipped cream mixture into the cooled panna cotta base. Pour into desired vessels and refrigerate until fully set, at least 4 hours.

Make huckleberry compote:
Add ¼ cup water, huckleberries, sugar, and cornstarch to a small pot and bring to a boil over high heat, stirring constantly.

Huckleberry Compote:

¼ cup water
1 cup huckleberries
3 tablespoons sugar
1 teaspoon cornstarch

Cook for 3 to 4 minutes or until desired thickness is reached. Transfer to a clean container and let cool in refrigerator.

Preheat oven to 375°F. Line a sheet tray with parchment paper. Spread the streusel crunch on the prepared tray. Bake for 4 to 5 minutes until golden brown. Let cool completely.

When panna cottas are set, dip vessels briefly into hot water to release them. Flip out onto plates and serve with spoonfuls of the huckleberry compote. Garnish with the streusel crunch.

Roasted Plum Chutney

MAKES 4 SERVINGS

When summer rolls around plums seem to overtake the markets. This roasted plum chutney is a great way to highlight and preserve the fruit past the summer months. It's not too sweet so the spicy flavors of cardamom and clove shine through. I like to serve this chutney as a dessert course with gouda cheese or over a scoop of cinnamon ice cream.

Directions

Preheat oven to 325°F. Combine the plums and remaining ingredients in a large bowl and toss well. Transfer to a 9-inch pie plate or baking dish and roast plums for 45 minutes to 1 hour, stirring every 15 minutes. Roast until liquid thickens and plums break down.

Remove cardamom pods, bay leaves, and cinnamon stick. Serve warm or chilled. Delicious served as a cheese accompaniment or over ice cream.

4 black plums, pitted and quartered

¼ cup brown sugar

2 cardamom pods

2 cloves, crushed

2 bay leaves

1 cinnamon stick

Glazed Pluots

MAKES 4 SERVINGS

1 cup sugar

4 tablespoons water

1 teaspoon fresh lemon
    juice

½ cup cognac

6 pluots, halved and
    pitted

Ice cream for serving
    (optional)

These glazed pluots are absolutely delectable and can be prepared in less than ten minutes. When cooked in the cognac caramel, the pluots release their juices, creating a deliciously sweet, gorgeous sauce that will blow your mind. It's the perfect ending to any farm-to-table summer meal.

Directions

Combine the sugar, water, and lemon juice in a medium pot over high heat. Let boil undisturbed until syrup begins to turn golden brown. Swirl pot to evenly caramelize the syrup. When amber color is achieved, remove from heat and stir in the cognac. Return to low heat and continue stirring until any seized sugar has dissolved. Add the pluots cut side down and cook for 1 minute. Gently flip them over and cook for 1 more minute. Delicious served hot or at room temperature.

Tomato Watermelon Pizza

MAKES 4–6 SERVINGS

This watermelon "pizza" is a refreshing dessert that show-cases exactly what farm-to-table is all about: fresh, seasonal ingredients that, when combined with minimal preparation, become food that is pure, flavorful, and satisfying.

Directions

Carefully cut cross-sectional slices of the watermelon. Lay one of the slices on a cutting board; set the others aside. Use a melon baller to create small indentations in the watermelon slice. Place the tomato halves cut side up in the indentations. Slice the mint leaves into thin strips and scatter them on top. Squeeze some fresh lemon juice over the "pizza." Sprinkle a little sea salt over each tomato half. Repeat with remaining watermelon slices. Serve immediately.

1 personal watermelon, chilled

1 pint cherry tomatoes, halved

1 bunch mint leaves

1 lemon, halved for juicing

Sea salt, for garnish

Lavender Shortbread

MAKES 1 (9-INCH) ROUND

½ cup unsalted butter, soft

¼ cup lavender sugar*

½ teaspoon vanilla extract

Pinch of salt

1 cup all-purpose flour

May and June are prime months for fresh lavender in California. This buttery shortbread beautifully encompasses lavender's relaxing fragrance and floral taste.

Directions

Preheat oven to 350°F. In a mixer fitted with the paddle attachment, cream the butter, lavender sugar, vanilla, and salt on medium speed for 2 minutes until light and fluffy. Add the flour and mix on low speed until just combined—mixture should be crumbly. Transfer to a 9-inch ungreased glass pie dish. Press dough down into the dish. Use a fork to poke holes on top and use the tines to mark the edges. Bake for 15 minutes until pale golden. Let cool slightly before turning out onto a cutting board. Use a sharp knife to slice the shortbread while still warm.

---

*When fresh lavender plants start appearing at the markets in May I like to make small batches of lavender sugar to give to my neighbors. Here's the simple recipe:

1 cup sugar

1 tablespoon finely chopped lavender leaves

Combine both ingredients in a bowl and store in an airtight jar. Sugar is ready to use in a few hours.

Mango Granita
MAKES 4-5 SERVINGS

So simple to make, this refreshing granita is great for those last-minute summer parties. Serve as is, or add to a glass of sparkling water for a cool dessert beverage.

Directions
Combine all ingredients in a blender and mix on high speed until mango is puréed. Pour mixture into a 9x13-inch baking dish. Place in freezer and stir every 20 to 30 minutes with a fork. Repeat until granita resembles crushed ice (about 4 more stirs). Granita keeps well in the freezer covered for a week.

4 ounces ripe mango, cubed

1⅓ cups filtered water

5 tablespoons sugar

1½ tablespoons dark rum

1 tablespoon fresh lemon juice

Mixed Berry Pavlovas

MAKES 5 PAVLOVAS

Pavlovas:

4 large egg whites, room
  temperature

1¼ cups sugar

2 teaspoons cornstarch

1 teaspoon vanilla extract

Mixed Berry Compote:

⅓ cup blueberries

⅓ cup blackberries

⅓ cup raspberries

⅓ cup sugar

Fresh mint and additional
  berries, for garnish

Blueberries, blackberries, and raspberries are cooked together to make a delicious compote that makes a stunning dessert when served over crisp meringues. The meringues are baked just long enough to have crisp exteriors and soft, billowy centers.

Make the pavlovas:

Preheat oven to 300°F. Line a sheet tray with parchment paper and set aside.

In a mixer fitted with the whip attachment, beat the whites on high speed until frothy. With the mixer still on, slowly add the sugar and beat until stiff, about 5 minutes. Remove bowl from mixer and fold in the cornstarch and vanilla. Use a large spoon to drop five mounds of meringue on the prepared sheet tray. Use the back of the spoon to form deep indentations in each center. Bake for 1 hour or until meringues easily pull off parchment and sound hollow when tapped on the bottom.

Make the berry compote:

While the meringues bake, combine all the compote ingredients in a medium pot over high heat. Stirring occasionally, boil the mixture until thickened, about 6 minutes. Set aside to cool.

To serve, place a spoonful of berry compote in the center of each meringue. Garnish with additional berries and fresh mint. Undressed meringues keep well in an airtight container for a week.

Black Mission Figs and Olive Oil Cake

MAKES 2 (6-INCH) CAKES

Fig season begins in early summer and this cake is a tasty way to celebrate its arrival. Fresh orange juice and zest gives the olive oil cake a nice pop that stands up well to the honeyed figs. This recipe makes two small cakes; freeze one for later and make half of the honeyed figs if you don't have many mouths to feed at one time.

Make the cake:

Preheat oven to 350°F. Line 2 (6-inch) round cake pans with parchment paper and grease well. Set aside.

Sift the flour, baking powder, baking soda, and salt. Set aside.

In a mixer fitted with the whip attachment, beat the eggs, sugar, milk, orange juice, zest, and vanilla on medium speed for 1 minute. Alternately add the dry ingredients with the olive oil in 3 portions, mixing well after each addition. Divide the batter into the prepared pans. Bake for 35 to 40 minutes or until an inserted toothpick comes out clean. Set aside to cool.

Make the figs:

Add the butter to a large sauté pan over medium heat. When butter begins to brown add the figs and cook for 1 to 2 minutes until soft, stirring occasionally. Remove from heat and stir in the honey and walnuts.

Cut off tops of the 2 cakes and spoon the honeyed figs and walnuts on top. I like to accompany slices of this cake with a dollop of crème fraîche.

Olive Oil Cake:

2 cups cake flour

1 teaspoon baking powder

½ teaspoon baking soda

¼ teaspoon salt

3 large eggs

1 cup sugar

½ cup whole milk

¼ cup orange juice

1 tablespoon orange zest

½ teaspoon vanilla extract

¾ cup olive oil

Honeyed Figs:

2 tablespoons salted butter

2 pounds fresh Black Mission figs, quartered

½ cup orange blossom honey

½ cup walnuts

White Fig Slab Pies

MAKES 6 PIES

1 cup all-purpose flour

½ tablespoon sugar

¼ teaspoon salt

6 tablespoons unsalted
    butter, cold and cubed

¼ cup ice water

¼ cup honey

6–7 white figs

2 tablespoons sugar, for
    sprinkling

These fig slab pies may be my favorite dessert in the book. They have a simple pâte brisée dough for the crust, which bakes up nice and crisp. The sweet, thin-skinned white figs are lightly sweetened with honey and sugar to create a sophisticated-tasting yet casual open-faced dessert.

Directions

Preheat oven to 400°F. Line a sheet tray with parchment paper and set aside.

Combine the flour, sugar, and salt in a mixer fitted with the paddle attachment. Add the butter and mix on low speed until butter breaks down to pea size. Add the ice water all at once and mix just until dough starts to come together. Remove from mixer and shape into a disc with your hands. Wrap with plastic and let chill 5 minutes in refrigerator.

On a floured surface, roll the dough out to a 12-inch square. Use a sharp knife to cut out 6 (3x5-inch) rectangles. Place on the prepared tray and poke holes in the dough with a fork. Use a mini offset spatula to spread the honey on the dough slabs.

Use a sharp knife to slice the figs and arrange them on the slabs. Sprinkle a teaspoon of sugar over each slab. Bake for 10 minutes, rotate, then 10 to 15 minutes more until golden brown on the edges.

Roasted Beet Panna Cotta with Candied Walnuts

MAKES ABOUT 3 CUPS

Beets may seem like an odd ingredient to use in a dessert, but if you're a fan of these root vegetables you will find this panna cotta absolutely heavenly. The beets are roasted first at high temperature then blended with cream, lemon, and sugar. The result is a delicious pudding-like dessert that boasts the most beautiful shade of fuchsia. Don't discard the beet greens as they are delicious sautéed with olive oil and garlic.

Make panna cotta:

Preheat oven to 400°F. Wrap each beet loosely in foil and roast for 1 hour on a baking sheet, or until tender enough for a paring knife to be easily inserted. Remove the beets from oven and set aside to cool slightly.

Stir together the gelatin and 2 tablespoons water in a small bowl. Let soften for 5 minutes.

Peel and discard the beet skins and place flesh in a blender along with 1 cup heavy cream. Purée until smooth.

Combine the remaining cream with the sugar and lemon juice in a large pot over medium heat. Warm until the cream becomes hot to touch but not boiling. Add the softened gelatin, remove from heat, and stir until dissolved. Add the puréed beet mixture to the pot and stir until combined. Pour into desired vessels and let chill completely before serving, at least 4 hours.

Make the candied walnuts:

Combine the walnuts and maple syrup in a sauté pan over medium heat. Cook the nuts, stirring constantly, until sugar dries and crystallizes, about 5 minutes. Transfer nuts to a piece of foil and set aside to cool.

To serve, garnish the panna cottas with candied walnuts.

Panna Cotta:

1 pound beets, de-stemmed and washed well

1 teaspoon powdered gelatin

2 tablespoons water

2 cups heavy cream

3 tablespoons sugar

2 teaspoons lemon juice

Candied Walnuts:

½ cup walnuts

¼ cup maple syrup

Key Lime Bars

MAKES 1 (8-INCH) SQUARE PAN

Crust:

1½ cups graham cracker
crumbs

6 tablespoons unsalted
butter, melted

2 tablespoons sugar

Filling:

4 ounces cream cheese,
room temperature

1 (14-ounce) can
condensed milk

½ cup key lime juice

2 teaspoons key lime zest

½ cup sweetened
coconut flakes

½ cup walnuts, chopped

½ cup butterscotch chips

½ cup semi-sweet
chocolate chips

Nothing tastes like summer to me more than key lime desserts. In this magic bar, a healthy dose of key lime juice and zest ensures that the tangy sweet flavor of summer shines through copious layers of walnuts, coconut, butterscotch, and chocolate.

Make the crust:

Preheat oven to 350°F. Line an 8-inch square pan with parchment paper and coat with pan spray. Combine the graham crumbs, butter, and sugar in a bowl and mix well with your hands. Transfer to the prepared pan and pat down well. Set aside.

Make the filling:

In a mixer fitted with the paddle attachment, beat the cream cheese on medium speed until smooth. Scrape the bowl well. Add the condensed milk, key lime juice, and zest and mix until incorporated, about 1 minute. Transfer to the prepared pan and smooth out top.

Combine the coconut, walnuts, butterscotch, and chocolate chips in a medium bowl. Sprinkle the mixture on top of the filling and gently press it down into the filling. Bake for 25 to 30 minutes or until filling is set. Cool completely in refrigerator before slicing.

Blueberry Zeppoles

MAKES ABOUT 18 ZEPPOLES

Zeppoles are Italy's version of deep-fried dough. They have a paper-thin exterior, spongy interior, and chewy texture. The blueberry sauce is perfect for dipping, filling, or drizzling. Plan accordingly as guests will likely eat way more than just one!

Make blueberry sauce:

Combine the blueberries, sugar, and water in a small pot over medium heat. Bring to a boil, stirring constantly. Continue cooking until sauce thickens and blueberries burst, about 7 to 8 minutes. Transfer to a clean bowl and set aside to cool.

Make zeppoles:

In a large bowl, whisk the eggs, sugar, and vanilla together. Add the flour, baking powder, and ricotta cheese and stir with a rubber spatula until ingredients are incorporated.

Fill a heavy bottomed pot (a Dutch oven works well) with peanut oil 2 inches deep and heat to 375°F. Use a small scoop to portion out the batter and fry for 3 to 4 minutes until golden brown and cooked through. Let zeppoles cool on a paper towel–lined plate. Repeat until all batter is fried.

Serve the zeppoles with the blueberry sauce or, if desired, pipe the sauce into their centers. Dust with powdered sugar before serving.

Blueberry Sauce:
1 cup blueberries
3 tablespoons sugar
2 tablespoons water

Zeppoles:
2 large eggs
¼ cup sugar
1 teaspoon vanilla extract
1 cup all-purpose flour
2 teaspoons baking powder
1 cup ricotta cheese
Peanut oil, for frying
Powdered sugar, for garnish

Cantaloupe Soup

MAKES ABOUT 4 SERVINGS

1 large cantaloupe, ripe and chilled

½ cup whole milk

2 teaspoons fresh lemon juice

1 teaspoon chopped cilantro, plus more for garnish

Agave to taste

Raspberries, for serving

This is a refreshing summer soup to make when cantaloupes are at their peak. I add a touch of cilantro and fresh lemon juice for flavor. I recommend serving the soup with some fresh raspberries; a perfect complement to cantaloupe.

Directions

Cut the cantaloupe in half and remove seeds. Cut the flesh into small pieces and place in a blender along with the milk, lemon juice, and cilantro. Purée until smooth. Add agave 1 teaspoon at a time until desired sweetness is reached. Strain soup and pour into bowls. Garnish with cilantro and serve with raspberries.

Mango and Passion Fruit with Warm Coconut Pudding

MAKES 4 SERVINGS

The tropical flavors of fresh mango, passion fruit, and coconut will no doubt transport you to somewhere warm and beautiful at first bite. The contrast of warm, creamy pudding with chilled, perfectly ripe, in-season fruit adds another delightful dimension.

Prepare the fruit:

Peel mangos and cut into thin slices. Transfer to a large plate. Peel and cut kiwis into thin slices and add to the plate. Slice passion fruits in half and remove seeds and pulp into a small bowl. Keep all the fruit in the refrigerator while you make the pudding.

Make the pudding:

Combine the milks and half the sugar in a medium pot. Add the remaining sugar, eggs, and cornstarch to a bowl, whisk well, and set aside. Bring the milk mixture to a boil over high heat. Slowly whisk a cup of the hot mixture into the eggs. Return liquid to pot and continue cooking over medium heat, stirring constantly. Let boil for 1 minute. Strain mixture into a clean bowl and whisk in the butter and vanilla. Serve warm with the prepared fruit.

Fruit:

1–2 ripe mangos

2 ripe kiwis

2 ripe passion fruits

Pudding:

8¾ ounces whole milk

4 ounces coconut milk

3 ounces sugar

2 large eggs

1 ounce cornstarch

1 ounce unsalted butter, soft

½ teaspoon pure vanilla extract

Blueberry Walnut Brownies

MAKES 1 (10-INCH) SQUARE PAN

4 ounces blueberries

1 teaspoon sugar

4 ounces unsalted butter

2 cups dark chocolate,
   rough chopped

2 large eggs

1 cup dark brown sugar

½ teaspoon vanilla
   extract

1 cup all-purpose flour

¾ cup walnuts, chopped

¼ cup cocoa powder,
   sifted

¼ teaspoon cinnamon

¼ teaspoon salt

Packed with a trifecta of superfood standouts, these blueberry walnut brownies with a hint of cinnamon are delicious *and* good for you. They are super fudgy, packed with decadent chocolate, crammed with juicy blueberries, and loaded with crunchy walnuts.

Directions

Preheat oven to 350°F. Grease a 10-inch square pan and set aside.

Rough chop the blueberries and combine them in a small bowl with 1 teaspoon of sugar. Set aside.

Melt the butter in a pot over medium heat. When completely melted, remove from heat and add the chopped chocolate. Stir until smooth and set aside.

In a mixer with the paddle attachment, beat the eggs, brown sugar, and vanilla on medium speed for 30 seconds. Mix in melted chocolate mixture. Add the flour, half of the walnuts, cocoa powder, cinnamon, and salt. Mix just until incorporated.

Spread the brownie batter in the prepared pan. Scatter spoonfuls of the blueberries on top followed by the remaining walnuts. Drag a paring knife through the batter to swirl the top.

Bake for 35 minutes. Remove from oven and let cool completely in the refrigerator before cutting.

Market Kettle Corn

Kettle corn is a popular treat at markets across the country. Kernels of corn are cooked with oil, sugar, and salt at a high temperature resulting in sweet and salty popcorn with a barely visible sugary crust. It's an irresistible snack that's delicious served warm or at room temperature. It is best served the day it's popped.

½ cup popcorn kernels
¼ cup peanut or
   vegetable oil
½ teaspoon salt
¼ cup sugar

Directions

Combine the kernels, oil, and salt in a medium pot over high heat. When the oil begins to sizzle, sprinkle the sugar over the kernels and cover with the lid. Shake the pot frequently until all the kernels have popped, about 3 minutes.

Strawberry Shortcake Roll

MAKES 1 ROLL (ABOUT 6 SERVINGS)

Roasted Strawberries:

1 pint strawberries, hulled
and quartered

¼ cup sugar

Jelly Roll Cake:

3 large eggs

1 cup sugar

¼ cup warm water

1 teaspoon pure vanilla
extract

¾ cup all-purpose flour

1 teaspoon baking
powder

¼ teaspoon salt

Powdered sugar for
sprinkling

Whipped Cream:

1 cup heavy cream

2 tablespoons sugar

1 teaspoon pure vanilla
extract

Garnish:

1 pint strawberries

I'll never forget the first time I made strawberry shortcake. I layered white sponge cake with generous spoonfuls of sweet whipped cream and slices of fresh strawberries. I admired it for a solid hour never imagining it would taste better than it looked. It was so simple yet blow-your-mind delicious. My farm-to-table version features my two favorite ways to eat strawberries: roasted and fresh. Roasted strawberries are spread onto a vanilla sponge cake and rolled up to create attractive serving slices; topped with whipped cream and fresh strawberries, this dessert is about as good as it gets.

Roast strawberries:

Preheat oven to 350°F. Combine the strawberries and sugar in a 9-inch pie pan. Roast in oven for 30 minutes. Remove from oven and use a potato masher or fork to break up the fruit. Return to oven and bake 15 minutes more. Break up fruit again and let cool on counter or in refrigerator. Fruit will thicken as it cools.

Make cake:

Adjust oven to 375°F. Line a half sheet pan with parchment paper and grease well. Set aside.

In a mixer fitted with the whip attachment, whisk the eggs and sugar on high speed for 5 minutes until thick. Add the warm water and vanilla on low speed. Add the flour, baking powder, and salt and mix on low speed just until incorporated. Spread evenly into prepared pan with a mini offset spatula.

Bake for 13 to 14 minutes, remove from oven, and run a knife around the edges. Flip out onto a piece of parchment paper that has been generously sprinkled with powdered sugar. Remove parchment from the underside and carefully roll up the cake from one of the narrow ends. Let cool completely, about 30 minutes.

Unroll the cake and spread the cooled roasted strawberry jam evenly onto the cake. Re-roll the cake and let set up in the refrigerator while you make the whipped cream.

Make cream:

In a mixer fitted with the whip attachment, whisk the heavy cream, sugar, and vanilla on high speed until medium peaks form. Slice the jelly roll and serve with whipped cream and slices of fresh strawberries.

Baked Papaya with Honeyed Curry Butter

MAKES 4 SERVINGS

Midway through summer, you'll start seeing papayas at the market. Ripe ones will yield to slight pressure and have amber orange skin. Don't fret if you can't score perfectly ripe ones at the market, as they mature quickly after few days at room temperature. In this recipe, the delicate floral flavor of papayas is enhanced when baked with honeyed curry butter.

Directions

Preheat oven to 350°F. Line a sheet tray with parchment paper. Slice the papayas in half and remove seeds. Place on prepared tray cut side up and set aside.

Melt the butter and honey in a small pot over low heat. Stir in the lime juice, zest, ginger, and curry powder. Brush the sauce over the papaya flesh. Reserve the remaining sauce for basting. Bake papayas for 40 minutes, basting every 10 minutes. Serve warm.

2 large papayas, ripe
2 ounces unsalted butter
2 tablespoons honey
1 tablespoon lime juice
1 teaspoon lime zest
1 teaspoon ground ginger
¼ teaspoon curry powder

AUTUMN

Seasonal Produce (September-December)

Acorn Squash

Apples

Asian Pear

Beets

Bell Peppers

Broccoli

Brussels Sprouts

Butternut Squash

Carrots

Cauliflower

Champagne Grapes

Concord Grapes

Corn

Crab Apples

Cranberries

Daikon

Elderberry

Endive

Figs

Grapefruit

Grapes

Green Beans

Guava

Huckleberries

Kumquats

Lettuce

Limes

Muscadine Grapes

Papaya

Pears

Persimmons

Pineapple

Pomegranate

Pumpkin

Quince

Radicchio

Radishes

Sweet Potatoes

Swiss Chard

Thomcord Grapes

Turnips

Recipes

Champagne Grape Cake

MAKES 1 (9-INCH) CAKE

Though more frequently seen on cheese plates, champagne grapes are actually quite lovely to bake with. They are intensely sweet and seedless berries that grow in tight clusters. Despite having delicate, thin skin these grapes retain their shape and juiciness even after baking. It takes patience to remove these tiny grapes from their stem but this yummy cake is well worth it!

Directions

Preheat oven to 350°F. Grease a 9-inch round pan and set aside.

In a mixer fitted with the paddle attachment, cream the butter and ¾ cup sugar on medium speed until light and fluffy, about 2 minutes. Add the egg and vanilla and beat for 2 minutes. Scrape bowl well. Add the flour, baking powder, baking soda, and salt. With the mixer on low, slowly pour in the buttermilk and mix until incorporated. Gently fold in the grapes with a rubber spatula. Spread batter in prepared pan and sprinkle top with 1 tablespoon sugar. Bake until inserted toothpick comes out clean, about 35 minutes.

4 ounces unsalted butter, soft

¾ cup plus 1 tablespoon sugar

1 large egg

1 teaspoon vanilla extract

2 cups all-purpose flour

1½ teaspoons baking powder

1 teaspoon baking soda

½ teaspoon salt

½ cup buttermilk

1½ cups Champagne grapes, de-stemmed

Thomcord Grape Crostata

MAKES 1 (10-INCH) CROSTATA

Filling:

1 tablespoon unsalted
    butter

1 pound Thomcord
    grapes, de-stemmed

5 tablespoons sugar

2 tablespoons cornstarch

Crust:

1¼ cups all-purpose flour

1 tablespoon lemon zest

½ teaspoon plus
    1 tablespoon sugar

½ teaspoon salt

6 ounces unsalted butter,
    cold and cubed

¼ cup ice water

Thomcord grapes are a hybrid of Thompson and Concord grapes. They have the flavor of Concords and the sweetness of Thompsons. In this recipe, the grapes are first cooked down into a thick jam that I guarantee will become your new favorite grape jam. Next, a buttery lemon dough is made and shaped to encase the Thomcord jam. Toasted walnuts pair nicely with this crostata.

Make the filling:

Melt the butter over medium heat in a large sauté pan. Cook the grapes in the butter for 10 minutes, stirring occasionally. Use a potato masher to break up the grapes and release their juices, stir in the sugar, and cook 5 minutes more. Strain the grapes through a mesh sieve over a large bowl. Press out as much juice as possible and discard skins. Pour the juice back into the pan, reserving ¼ cup in the bowl. Whisk the cornstarch into the reserved liquid and add it to the pot over medium heat. Bring to a boil and cook for 1 minute. Remove from heat and let mixture cool while you prepare the crust.

Make crust:

Preheat oven to 375°F. Coat the bottom and sides of a 10-inch springform pan with nonstick spray and set aside.

In a mixing bowl fitted with the paddle attachment, mix the flour, lemon zest, ½ teaspoon sugar, and salt. Add the butter and mix on low speed until butter breaks down to pea size. Add the ice water all at once and mix just until dough starts coming together. Form into a disk with lightly floured hands, wrap with plastic, and refrigerate for 5 minutes to chill.

On a lightly floured surface, roll out the dough to a ¼-inch thick circle, roughly 14 inches in diameter. Drape over the prepared pan and gently press the dough into the bottom and up along the sides. Prick the bottom with a fork. Refrigerate for 10 minutes to chill.

Pour the grape jam into the chilled dough. Trim the edges of the dough so they are three-quarters of the way up the sides. It's okay if the sides are not even; you want a rustic look. Gently fold the dough over the filling in an overlapping pattern. Sprinkle 1 tablespoon sugar over the crust. Bake until filling is set and crust is golden brown, about 25 to 30 minutes. Let cool completely before slicing.

Fried Fuji Apple Pies
MAKES ABOUT 7 PIES

These fried apple pies are crazy good. Their buttery cinnamon crust is delicate and flaky, making it the perfect shell for the moist caramel-infused apple filling. Though delicious served right after frying, these pies are just as good when eaten at room temperature.

Make topping:

Peel the apples and cut them into ⅛-inch thick slices. Cut each slice into quarters and set aside. Add the sugar and water to a medium pot over high heat. Let the mixture cook undisturbed until it begins to turn golden brown. Stir to ensure even coloring at this point and then add the chopped apples and butter. The sugar will seize briefly but will melt as the apples release their juices. Stirring continuously, cook the fruit for about 5 minutes until they soften. Set aside.

Make the dough:

Combine the flour, sugar, cinnamon, and salt in a mixer fitted with the paddle attachment. Add the butter and mix on low speed until butter breaks down to pea size. Add the ice water all at once and mix just until dough starts to come together. Remove from mixer and shape into a disc with your hands. Wrap with plastic and refrigerator for 5 minutes to chill.

On a floured surface, roll the dough out to ⅛-inch thickness. Use a 3-inch round cutter to portion out the dough and place on a parchment-lined sheet tray. Re-roll scraps as necessary and repeat this step with remaining dough. Place a tablespoon of the cooked apples in the center of each round, wet the edges lightly with water, and fold over the bottom halves of each to create a half moon shape. Press the edges together and crimp to seal. Place the pies in the refrigerator while the oil heats.

Fill a heavy bottomed pot (a Dutch oven works well) with 1-inch deep peanut oil. Heat the oil to 375°F. Carefully drop the pies in the oil and fry until golden brown, about 4 minutes per side. Use a slotted spoon to remove the pies and let them drain on paper towels. Delicious served warm or at room temperature. Garnish with powdered sugar before serving.

Filling:

2 large Fuji apples

½ cup sugar

¼ cup water

1 tablespoon unsalted butter

Dough:

1 cup all-purpose flour

½ tablespoon sugar

¼ teaspoon cinnamon

¼ teaspoon salt

6 tablespoons unsalted butter, cold and cubed

¼ cup ice water

Peanut oil, for frying

Powdered sugar, for garnish

White Chocolate Grapefruit Pots de Crème

MAKES 3 SERVINGS

1 cup heavy cream

¼ cup whole milk

1 large grapefruit

8 ounces white
   chocolate, chopped

4 large egg yolks

¼ teaspoon salt

At my first restaurant job out of culinary school, I was in charge of baking three types of pots de crème. I tediously had to bake them in water baths in a multi-deck oven. Without fail, some were done before others, requiring me to carefully remove them from the oven without knocking over or dripping water on the others. It was a terrible task I dreaded every night. I've since discovered that the simplest, most consistent, and efficient way to prepare pots de crème is by cooking the custard over the stove rather than baking it. In these pots de crème, I use the zest of one large grapefruit to flavor the custard, which is rounded out with a healthy dose of white chocolate.

Directions

Prepare an ice bath and set aside.

Combine the cream and milk in a small pot and warm it over medium heat. Remove from heat, stir in the zest of one grapefruit, cover, and set aside.

In a double boiler, melt the white chocolate over simmering water. Whisk in the yolks and salt. Remove the bowl and add the cream mixture a little at a time, whisking gently after each addition. Return bowl to the double boiler and continue stirring until mixture reaches 160°F. Place bowl over the ice bath and cool to 90°F, stirring occasionally.

Divide the custard into 3 (¾-cup) ramekins, cover with plastic, and let set up in refrigerator for at least 4 hours. Serve with grapefruit segments.

Pineapple Sorbet

MAKES 4-6 SERVINGS

I'm always drawn to fresh pineapple at the market but when I get home I can't seem to eat too much of it at a time. But pineapple sorbet? I can eat the whole batch! This sorbet is lively and bright with a tinge of cinnamon, clove, and thyme.

Directions

Combine 2 cups filtered water and the sugar in a medium pot over high heat. Bring to a boil, stirring until sugar is dissolved. Remove from heat and add the cloves, thyme, and cinnamon. Cover and let steep 5 minutes.

Use a serrated knife to remove the top and bottom of the pineapple. Carefully slice the skin off, making sure to cut deep enough to remove the eyes. Cut the pineapple into small pieces and place in a blender.

Strain the sugar mixture into the blender and purée until smooth. Press the mixture through a mesh sieve into a clean container and discard pulp. Place the sorbet base in the refrigerator until completely chilled. Spin in an ice cream maker. Let set up in the freezer if you prefer a firmer consistency.

2 cups filtered water

1½ cups sugar

6 cloves, crushed

2 thyme springs

½ stick cinnamon

1 large pineapple, ripe

Honey-Roasted Pineapple

MAKES 4 SERVINGS

1 large pineapple, ripe

¼ cup brown sugar

¼ cup orange blossom
   honey

¼ cup orange juice (fresh,
   please)

1 teaspoon vanilla extract

Gelato, ice cream, or
   yogurt, for serving

The trick to making these honey-roasted pineapple wedges uber-delicious is having the patience to cook them long enough for a nice, deep caramelization to occur. They are delicious served with coconut gelato.

Directions

Use a serrated knife to remove the top and bottom of the pineapple. Carefully slice the skin off, making sure to cut deep enough to remove the eyes. Cut the pineapple into 8 wedges and place them in a zippered bag.

Whisk together the brown sugar, honey, orange juice, and vanilla in a large bowl. Pour into the zippered bag, seal well, and shake to coat. Let fruit marinate for 10 minutes.

Preheat oven to 425°F and place a cast-iron pan on the middle rack. When oven is ready, place the pineapple wedges into the pan and roast for 10 minutes on each side, occasionally basting with the leftover marinade. Continue roasting the fruit, checking every 5 minutes, until the fruit is nicely caramelized on all sides. Delicious served with coconut gelato.

Apple Pine Nut Cakes with Salted Caramel Frosting

MAKES 14 CAKES

Grated Gala apples, including their fibrous skins, give these little cakes a hearty, earthy flavor. The addition of tiny pine nuts adds a soft crunch. The old-fashioned salted caramel frosting adds just the right amount of sweetness.

Make the cake:

Preheat oven to 350°F. Grease two cupcake pans well and set aside.

Grate 3 cups' worth of apples with their skin on and place them in a large bowl. Let sit for 10 minutes to allow water to drain from them.

In a mixer fitted with the whisk attachment, beat the sugars, oil, butter, and vanilla until blended. Add the eggs and mix well. Squeeze out any remaining water from the apples and add them to the egg mixture. Mix until incorporated. Add the flour, pine nuts, apple pie spice, baking powder, baking soda, and salt and mix for 1 minute on medium speed. Scrape bowl well. Use a large ice cream scoop to portion out the batter, filling each cup two-thirds full. Bake for 25 to 30 minutes until centers are set.

Make the frosting:

When cakes are completely cool, make the frosting. Combine the brown sugar and butter in a small pot and cook over high heat until sugar is dissolved, stirring constantly. Stir in the milk and bring to a boil. Cook for 2 minutes. Pour mixture into a mixer fitted with the paddle attachment. Add the powdered sugar and salt. Mix on low speed until incorporated, then increase to high speed and beat for 1 minute. Let the mixture cool for a couple minutes and then transfer frosting to a piping bag. Decorate the cakes as desired. Pipe briskly, as the frosting sets up quickly!

Cake:

5 large Gala apples

1 cup sugar

½ cup brown sugar

½ cup vegetable oil

¼ cup unsalted butter, melted

1 teaspoon vanilla extract

2 large eggs

2 cups all-purpose flour

½ cup pine nuts

2 teaspoons apple pie spice

1 teaspoon baking powder

1 teaspoon baking soda

½ teaspoon salt

Salted Caramel Frosting:

1 cup brown sugar

½ cup unsalted butter, soft

¼ cup whole milk

2 cups powdered sugar, sifted

½ teaspoon salt

Pomegranate Chocolate Cookies

MAKES ABOUT 2 DOZEN COOKIES

1 large pomegranate

1 cup unsalted butter, soft

1½ cups sugar

1 teaspoon vanilla extract

2 large eggs

2½ cups all-purpose flour

2 cups semi-sweet mini chocolate chips

⅔ cup unsweetened cocoa powder

1 teaspoon baking soda

¼ teaspoon salt

These fudgy chocolate cookies are a pretty and delicious way to showcase pomegranates when they begin appearing in the autumn months. The pomegranate arils remain red and crunchy even after baking. Pomegranates are nutrient-rich and a powerful antioxidant so you can feel good about eating these decadent delights.

Directions

Preheat oven to 350°F. Line two baking trays with parchment paper and set aside.

De-seed the pomegranate and set aside 1 cup's worth of arils. Refrigerate or freeze extra arils.

In a mixer fitted with the paddle attachment, cream the butter, sugar, and vanilla on medium speed until fluffy, about 2 minutes. Add the eggs one at a time, mixing well after each addition. Scrape bowl well. Add the remaining ingredients including the pomegranate arils. Mix on low speed until combined.

Use a 1-ounce scoop to portion out the dough onto the prepared trays. Press dough down slightly. Bake for 10 minutes. Let cool completely before serving.

Dulce de Leche Cheesecake with Fuji Apples

MAKES 4 INDIVIDUAL CHEESECAKES

The flavors of this dulce de leche cheesecake are all about autumn. It's topped with caramelized apples and drizzled with warm, gooey dulce de leche. Because it is baked without a water bath, this dessert's texture is similar to that of dense New York style cheesecakes.

Crust:
1½ cups graham crumbs
¼ cup unsalted butter, melted

Filling:
2 (8-ounce) packages cream cheese, room temperature
1 (13.4-ounce) can Nestle La Lechera Dulce de Leche
1½ tablespoons all-purpose flour
⅛ teaspoon salt
1 cup sugar
2 large eggs

Topping:
2 large apples
½ cup plus 1 teaspoon sugar
¼ cup water
1 tablespoon unsalted butter
½ cup sliced almonds

Directions

Preheat oven to 350°F. Grease 4 (¾-cup) ramekins and set aside.

Make crust:

Combine the graham crumbs and butter in a bowl and mix well. Divide the mixture evenly into each ramekin. Press the mixture onto the bottom and up the sides about 1-inch high. Place in refrigerator.

Make filling:

In a mixer fitted with the paddle attachment, beat the cream cheese on medium speed until smooth. Add half the can of dulce de leche, flour, and salt. Mix until incorporated. Scrape bowl well and beat in the sugar. Scrape bowl well. Add the eggs one at a time, mixing well after each addition. Pour batter into prepared ramekins. Bake for 25 minutes. Let set up in refrigerator for at least 2 hours.

Make toppings:

Peel the apples and cut them into ⅛-inch thick slices. Cut each slice into quarters. Add the ½ cup sugar and ¼ cup water to a medium pot over high heat. Let the mixture cook undisturbed until it begins to turn golden brown. Stir to ensure even coloring at this point and then add the chopped apples and butter. The sugar will seize briefly but will melt as the apples release their juice. Stirring continuously, cook the fruit for about 5 minutes until softened. Set aside.

Place the almonds and 1 teaspoon sugar in a small sauté pan over medium heat. Agitate the almonds as they toast. Continue cooking until the almonds are golden brown. Transfer to a plate and set aside.

Dip the bottom of the ramekins in 1-inch deep hot water for 15 seconds. Run a paring knife around the edges, flip out cheesecakes, and place on serving dishes. Top with the apples and almonds. Whisk the remaining dulce de leche with 1 to 2 tablespoons hot water until desired consistency is reached. Drizzle over cheesecakes before serving.

Sweet Potato Pie

MAKES 1 (9-INCH) PIE

This creamy vegetable pie is a true Southern specialty. I add just a touch of vanilla and cinnamon to flavor the sweet potato, but not too much so its earthy essence isn't lost. Try making this pie during Thanksgiving as an alternative to pumpkin pie . . . or, actually, make both!

Make crust:

Combine the flour, salt, and sugar in a mixing bowl with the paddle attachment. Add the cubed butter and mix on medium speed until pea size. Add the ice water and mix just until dough starts coming together. Gather into a ball with your hands and shape into a disc. Wrap with plastic and chill in refrigerator for 10 minutes.

Roll out the dough on a lightly floured surface to a 12-inch circle and line a 9-inch pie plate. Trim and flute the edges, prick holes in the dough with a fork, and place in refrigerator to chill for 10 minutes.

Preheat oven to 350°F. Whisk the egg white and brush a thin layer on the bottom of the pie shell. Bake for 7 minutes and let cool on counter while you make the filling. Increase the oven temperature to 400°F.

Make filling:

In a large bowl, whisk the eggs, sugar, and sweet potato. Add the milk, butter, vanilla, and cinnamon. Mix until incorporated. Pour into pie shell and bake for 10 minutes. Reduce oven temperature to 325°F and bake for 30 minutes more until center is set.

*Bake one large pierced sweet potato directly on your middle oven rack in a 400°F oven for 45 to 60 minutes until cooked through.

Crust:

1¼ cups all-purpose flour

½ teaspoon salt

½ teaspoon sugar

4 ounces unsalted butter, cold and cubed

3 tablespoons ice water

1 large egg white

Filling:

2 large eggs

⅔ cup sugar

1 cup baked, mashed sweet potato*

¾ cup evaporated milk

1 tablespoon salted butter, melted

½ teaspoon vanilla extract

½ teaspoon cinnamon

Grapefruit in Citrus Mint Syrup

MAKES 2 SERVINGS

½ cup fresh orange juice

1 tablespoon sugar

1 teaspoon fresh lemon juice

10 mint leaves plus 2 sprigs for garnish

1 large grapefruit

This is a lovely way to serve fresh grapefruit. It's served with a light citrus mint syrup that is simple and refreshing.

Directions

In a medium bowl, whisk the orange juice, sugar, and lemon juice together. Tear 10 mint leaves into small pieces and whisk them into the juice mixture. Set bowl aside while you prep the grapefruit.

Use a sharp knife to remove the grapefruit's skin and pith. Slice cross-sectional pieces and divide them between two bowls. Strain the citrus mint syrup and pour it over the grapefruit slices. Garnish with mint sprigs and serve immediately.

Quince Brown Butter Tart

MAKES 1 (9½-INCH) TART

Quince Filling:

1½ pounds (about 3–4 large) quince

½ cup sugar

1 teaspoon lemon juice

6 cloves, crushed

1 cinnamon stick

2 tablespoons unsalted butter

Crust:

1 cup all-purpose flour

½ tablespoon sugar

¼ teaspoon salt

6 tablespoons unsalted butter, cold and cubed

¼ cup ice water

Brown Butter Custard:

5 ounces unsalted butter

3 large eggs

1 cup brown sugar

1 teaspoon vanilla extract

⅓ cup all-purpose flour

I like to make this autumn-inspired tart over the course of two days. Cooking the quince takes a fair amount of love and patience so I don't like to rush this step. Plus, cooked quince releases a ridiculously beautiful aroma that I like to let linger in my loft for a full day. I prefer serving this tart chilled.

Make the quince:

Peel the quince and cut them into small ¼-inch cubes. Add to a large sauté pan with the sugar, lemon juice, cloves, and cinnamon. Place pan over high heat and bring to a boil. Reduce heat, bring to a gentle simmer, and cover. Cook for 1 hour, stirring occasionally. After an hour, you will notice the liquid has evaporated. Stir in the butter and cook uncovered for 5 minutes more, stirring frequently to prevent scorching. Remove from heat and let cool.

Make the crust:

Preheat oven to 375°F. Combine the flour, sugar, and salt in a mixer fitted with the paddle attachment. Add the butter and mix on low speed until butter breaks down to pea size. Add the ice water all at once and mix just until dough starts to come together. Remove from mixer and shape into a disc with your hands. Wrap with plastic and let chill 5 minutes in refrigerator.

On a floured surface, roll the dough out to an 11-inch circle. Line the bottom and sides of a 9½-inch tart pan with the dough. Poke holes on the bottom with a fork. Lay a large piece of parchment paper with overhang over the tart pan and fill with baking beans or pie weights. Bake for 15 minutes. Remove from oven, carefully remove the beans and parchment, and let cool on counter while you make the custard.

Make the brown butter custard:

Place the butter in a small pot over medium heat. Cook the butter until it begins to brown, about 10 minutes. Stir occasionally to prevent scorching. Remove from heat and set aside.

In a large bowl, whisk the eggs, brown sugar, and vanilla. Add the flour and whisk until incorporated. Whisk in the browned butter. Stir in the cooked quince and pour mixture into the par-baked tart shell. Bake for 30 to 35 minutes until filling is set and slightly puffy. Let cool completely in refrigerator before slicing and serve chilled.

Pear Cake

MAKES 1 (9-INCH) ROUND CAKE

Autumn and winter are peak seasons for pear varietals. I like to use Bosc in this cake recipe but feel free to experiment with other types. I love this cake because it presents pears in two delicious ways: the caramelized pear layer on top, and the fresh chunks of pear nestled in the cake. The olive oil cake has a flavorful blend of cardamom, clove, orange, and vanilla that complements pear nicely.

Directions

Preheat oven to 350°F. Grease a 9-inch round cake pan and set aside.

Combine the milk, cardamom, and cloves in a small pot over high heat. Bring to just a boil, remove from heat, and let steep.

In another small pot, combine the brown sugar, butter, and 1 teaspoon vanilla over high heat. Boil for 30 seconds, stirring constantly, and then pour into the prepared cake pan. Tilt the pan to ensure the caramel evenly coats the bottom.

Peel the pears and cut them in half. Remove cores and cut ⅛-inch thick slices. Arrange them on the bottom of the caramel-coated pan in a concentric pattern. Rough chop the remaining pears, enough to measure 1 cup, and set aside.

In a large bowl, whisk the egg, sugar, oil, orange zest, and 1 teaspoon vanilla extract. Strain in the infused milk and stir in until blended. Add the flour, baking powder, baking soda, salt, and chopped pears. Stir until all the ingredients are incorporated. Pour batter into the pan and smooth out top. Bake for 25 minutes until the center is set. Let cake cool for a few minutes before inverting onto a serving plate.

⅓ cup whole milk

6 cardamom pods, crushed

2 cloves, crushed

⅓ cup brown sugar

¼ cup salted butter

2 teaspoons vanilla extract

2 large Bosc pears

1 large egg

⅓ cup sugar

¼ cup olive oil

1 teaspoon orange zest

¾ cup all-purpose flour

1½ teaspoons baking powder

¾ teaspoon baking soda

¼ teaspoon salt

Bartlett Pear Sorbet

MAKES 6 SERVINGS

6 Bartlett pears, very
   ripe
2 cups water
1 cup sugar
1 tablespoon lemon juice

This pear sorbet is super smooth and has a luscious and creamy consistency. I recommend using overripe pears to ensure the beautiful flavor of pear shines through. Bartletts are my pear of choice for this sorbet, as they are incredibly juicy and buttery.

Directions

Peel, core, and quarter the pears. Place in a pot along with the water, sugar, and lemon juice. Bring to a boil over high heat and then reduce heat and let simmer until fruit is tender, about 20 minutes. Transfer mixture to a clean bowl and place over an ice bath. When cool, purée in a blender and strain. Spin in an ice cream maker and store in freezer.

Pumpkin Ginger Tart

MAKES 1 (9½-INCH) TART

My lovely neighbor Donna is a prolific pumpkin grower. Luckily for me, she is also incredibly generous. As a result, I get to make and eat more than my fair share of pumpkin dishes throughout the year. This pumpkin tart is one of my favorites. It's incredibly easy to make and has a nice mellow pumpkin flavor with a hint of ginger.

Roast the pumpkin:

Preheat oven to 375°F. Slice off the top of the pumpkin and discard. Use a large spoon to remove the seeds and stringy flesh. Cut the pumpkin into 1-inch slices, toss them in a large bowl with the olive oil, and season with salt. Place the pumpkin on a foil-lined sheet tray and roast for 40 minutes, or until flesh is soft. Remove from oven and set aside to cool.

Make the crust:

Reduce oven temperature to 350°F. Combine the gingersnaps and butter in a medium bowl and press into the bottom and sides of a 9½-inch tart pan. Bake for 10 minutes.

Make the filling:

Using a sharp knife, carefully cut away the pumpkin flesh from its skin. Place the flesh in a blender and purée until no chunks remain. In a large bowl, whisk 2 cups of the puréed pumpkin with the egg, sour cream, sugar, ginger, and cinnamon. Pour into the tart shell. Bake for 20 minutes or until filling is set. Cool completely before serving.

Roasted Pumpkin:
1 small (5-pound) pumpkin
1 tablespoon olive oil
Salt

Gingersnap Crust:
2 cups crushed gingersnaps
¼ cup unsalted butter, melted

Filling:
1 large egg
½ cup sour cream
¼ cup sugar
1 teaspoon fresh ginger, minced
1 teaspoon cinnamon

Kumquat Malasadas

MAKES 12 MALASADAS

1½ teaspoons active dry
    yeast
1 teaspoon plus ¼ cup
    sugar
2 tablespoons warm
    water
2 cups all-purpose flour
½ teaspoon nutmeg
¼ teaspoon salt
2 large eggs
½ cup (about 3 ounces)
    kumquats, seeded and
    finely chopped
⅓ cup whole milk
2 tablespoons unsalted
    butter, melted
½ teaspoon vanilla
    extract
Peanut oil for frying
Sugar for coating

Malasadas are traditional Portuguese donuts that are widely seen in Hawaii. My farm-to-table version includes fresh kumquats, nutmeg, and vanilla. As a result, they are mildly sweet, slightly tangy, and irresistibly good. Lighter than donuts found on the mainland, they have a crispy exterior and a soft, squishy interior. As with most fried delicacies, these are best served the day they are made. You'll need a heavy bottomed pot (a Dutch oven works well) and thermometer for this one.

Directions

Stir together the yeast and sugar with the warm water to activate yeast. Set aside. Combine the flour, nutmeg, and salt in a mixer fitted with the paddle attachment.

In a separate bowl, whisk together the eggs, kumquats, milk, sugar, butter, and vanilla. Add to the dry ingredients and mix on low speed until a smooth dough forms. Transfer dough to a clean, oiled bowl and cover with a dish towel. Let rise in a warm spot until the mixture doubles in size, about 1 hour.

Line a sheet tray with parchment paper and coat well with pan spray. Use the pan spray to oil your hands well and punch down the dough. Pinch off golf sized pieces of dough and place on the prepared sheet tray. Re-oil your hands as necessary. You should end up with 12 pieces of dough. Coat the tops of the dough with pan spray, cover with a dish towel, and place in a warm spot to rise while you prepare the frying oil.

Fill a Dutch oven or a heavy high sided pan with peanut oil 2 inches deep. Place over high heat until oil reaches 350°F. Use scissors to cut parchment squares around each piece of dough. Gently scrape off 3 to 4 dough balls into the oil and discard the parchment squares. Fry until they are golden brown all over, about 1½ minutes per side. Remove from oil and place the malasadas on a plate lined with paper towels. Repeat until all the malasadas are fried. Place about 2 cups of sugar in a large zippered bag. Transfer the malasadas two at a time to the bag, seal, and shake well until evenly coated with sugar. Serve that day.

Roasted Grapes Bruschetta

MAKES ABOUT 5-6 SERVINGS

One of my favorite snacks is red grapes. The combination of a thin crisp skin and soft flesh with a burst of sweet juice is deeply satisfying. Sometimes though, a greater need calls. Roasting them is the answer. It's a sophisticated option for turning grapes into a farm-to-table dessert. I like to serve the roasted grapes on sweet bread that is topped with a slather of crème fraîche; a dessert bruschetta of sorts. Serving the grapes warm provides a nice contract to the cool crème fraîche. I often accompany this dish with aged gouda as a dessert cheese course.

Make the bruschetta:

Preheat oven to 350°F. Line two sheet trays with parchment paper and set aside.

Spread the butter over the baguette slices and generously sprinkle with sugar. Place them on one of the sheet trays and bake for 8 to 10 minutes, or until lightly toasted. Set aside to cool while you roast the grapes.

Make the grapes:

Adjust oven temperature to 450°F. Place the grapes in a large bowl. Add the oil, butter, and sugar. Gently coat the grapes well and place them on the prepared sheet tray. Bake for 10 to 11 minutes or until skins begin to blister.

Spread some crème fraîche on the toasts. Top with the roasted grapes and serve immediately.

Bruschetta:
¼ cup unsalted butter, soft
1 small baguette, cut into ½-inch thick slices
2–3 tablespoons sugar

Roasted Grapes:
1 pound red grapes, cut into small bunches
1 tablespoon canola oil
1 tablespoon unsalted butter, melted
1 tablespoon sugar
¾ cup crème fraîche or sour cream

Baked Granny Smith Apples

MAKES 4 SERVINGS

Baked Apples:

4 medium Granny Smith apples

2 tablespoons unsalted butter

2 tablespoons honey

½ cup dark brown sugar

½ cup currants

½ cup walnuts, finely chopped

1 teaspoon cinnamon

⅛ teaspoon salt

Butterscotch Sauce:

½ cup dark brown sugar

3 tablespoons unsalted butter

⅓ cup heavy cream

When apples start appearing at the market, it's a sure sign that autumn has arrived. One of the first dishes I make to welcome in the season is a classic: baked apples. I like to use the Granny Smith variety for this recipe. Its tartness is balanced with a filling that consists of walnuts and currants sweetened with honey and brown sugar. The homemade butterscotch sauce is optional but I highly recommend it.

Make baked apples:

Preheat oven to 375°F.

Slice off the top third of the apples and set aside tops. Use a melon baller to scoop out the flesh from the bottoms, leaving a ½-inch thick edge from the skin. Place apples in a small rimmed baking dish that fits the apples snugly.

Melt the butter and honey over low heat in a medium pot. Remove from heat and add the remaining ingredients. Stir until incorporated. Use a small spoon to fill the apple cavities with the brown sugar mixture. Place the apple tops on. Fill the dish ¼-inch deep with warm water. Bake 40 minutes.

Make butterscotch sauce:

Cook the brown sugar and butter in a small pot over medium heat, stirring constantly. After boiling for 5 minutes, stir in the cream. Cook for 2 more minutes to thicken sauce. Serve warm with the baked apples.

Kumquat Poppers
MAKES 20 POPPERS

These bite-sized poppers are tangy sweet delights that melt in your mouth and let you taste what a kumquat is all about. A citrus mousse is piped into hollowed out kumquats and then frozen for a delicious treat on a warm day. If they have been kept in the freezer for awhile, let them sit at room temperature for 5 minutes before serving.

20 kumquats
1 clementine
2 tablespoons Cointreau
2 tablespoons sugar
1 large egg, separated
¼ cup heavy cream

Directions

Line a flat plate or sheet tray with parchment paper and set aside.

Cut off the bottoms of all the kumquats so that only a little flesh is exposed and each kumquat can stand erect. Slice off a slightly larger portion on the other end of each kumquat and discard the cut tops. Over a medium-sized bowl, use your thumb to scrape out the flesh of 10 kumquats, running your thumb along the inside of the rind. Make sure the bowl beneath catches as much juice and flesh as possible. Repeat with the remaining 10 kumquats, this time discarding the juice and flesh. Stand the 20 kumquats upright on the prepared plate and place in refrigerator to chill.

Slice the clementine in half and squeeze as much juice as you can into the kumquat bowl. Transfer the juice and flesh from the bowl to a medium pot. Add the Cointreau and 1 tablespoon sugar. Place over medium heat and stir until sugar is dissolved and juice simmers. Return sweetened juice to the bowl and set aside.

Bring a pot of water to a gentle simmer. Place the juice bowl over the pot and whisk in the egg yolk. Continue whisking until mixture thickens and is hot to touch. Remove bowl and place the mousse base in the freezer to cool.

In another large bowl, whisk the heavy cream to stiff peaks. Gently fold the cream partially into the mousse base (you want some white streaks to still be visible) and return it to the freezer. In the same bowl you used for the cream, whisk the egg white and 1 tablespoon sugar to medium-stiff peaks. Gently fold the meringue into the mousse. Transfer to a piping bag and fill the kumquat shells. Place in freezer until poppers are completely set, about 45 minutes.

Lady Alice Apple Tarte Tatin

MAKES 1 (12-INCH) TARTE TATIN

1 sheet frozen puff pastry (I prefer Pepperidge Farm)

4 Lady Alice apples, peeled and cored

3 tablespoons unsalted butter

¾ cup sugar

1 teaspoon lemon juice

½ teaspoon salt

½ teaspoon vanilla extract

One of the biggest complaints I hear about tarte tatin is that the pastry crust always comes out too soggy. I've learned the best way to avoid this is to cook the apples first to remove any excess liquid. Then place a par-baked puff pastry round on top of the cooked apples before finishing the whole tatin in the oven. This ensures a crispy crust topped with candy-like apples and a luscious caramel sauce. I like to use Lady Alice apples in this recipe because they keep their shape and texture well when cooked at high temperatures. Cultivated in Washington state, they have a complex sweet tart flavor and a beautiful yellow and rosy blush hue.

Directions

Preheat oven to 375°F. Thaw the puff pastry at room temperature. Roll out to ⅛-inch thick on a lightly floured surface. Cut out a 12-inch circle and discard scraps. Place the circle on a parchment-lined sheet tray and keep in the refrigerator.

Cut each apple into 8 even wedges and place in a bowl. Set aside. In an ovenproof 10-inch skillet, melt the butter over medium heat. Stir in the sugar, lemon juice, salt, and vanilla. Let simmer 1 minute undisturbed. Cook for 2 more minutes, stirring continuously. At this point, you'll notice the caramel turn a dark amber. Carefully stir in the apple slices. Cook for 20 to 25 minutes, stirring occasionally, until the liquid cooks off. While the apples cook, remove the puff pastry from the refrigerator and bake for 20 minutes.

When the apples are cooked and the caramel is dry, remove from heat. Use tongs to arrange the apple wedges in a spiral pattern. Place the baked puff pastry round on top and place the pan in the oven for 20 minutes. Remove from oven and let sit for 15 minutes before flipping out onto a serving plate.

WINTER

Seasonal Produce (January-March)

Bananas	Kumquats
Beets	Leeks
Blood Orange	Lemon
Broccoli	Lime
Brussels Sprouts	Mandarin Oranges
Buttercup Squash	Meyer Lemons
Carrots	Mustard Greens
Cauliflower	Oranges
Clementines	Passion Fruit
Coconut	Pear
Collard Greens	Persimmons
Cranberry	Pummelo
Dates	Red Currants
Endive	Sweet Potatoes
Grapefruit	Tangelos
Grapes	Tangerines
Kale	Turnips
Kiwi	Winter Squash

Recipes

Blood Orange Napoleon

MAKES 4 SERVINGS

1 sheet frozen puff pastry
(I prefer Pepperidge
Farm)

2 tablespoons powdered
sugar

¼ cup cornstarch

2 large eggs

½ cup sugar

2 cups whole milk

1 tablespoon unsalted
butter, soft

1 teaspoon vanilla extract

1 teaspoon finely grated
blood orange zest

4–6 blood oranges,
segmented

Powdered sugar, for
garnish

My favorite winter fruit is the blood orange. It has a unique sweet tart flavor with berry undertones. Moreover, I love how its flesh can range from a deep purple to a rosy red to a bright orange. In my opinion, blood oranges are best enjoyed fresh, which is why I love making this napoleon-inspired dessert. Layers of citrus pastry cream and flaky caramelized puff pastry are separated by fresh blood orange segments, creating a medley of appealing textures.

Directions

Preheat oven to 325°F. Remove puff pastry from freezer and let thaw at room temperature. Line a sheet tray with parchment paper and set aside.

Roll the thawed puff pastry sheet on a lightly floured surface to a 10x14-inch rectangle. Place onto prepared sheet, poke holes in the dough with a fork, and top with a sheet of parchment. Place another sheet tray on top and bake for 40 minutes or until pastry is baked through. Remove from oven and turn oven to high broil.

Remove top sheet tray and parchment. Sift 1 tablespoon powdered sugar over the dough and bake for 1 to 2 minutes until sugar caramelizes. Remove from oven and carefully flip over the puff pastry. Again, sprinkle 1 tablespoon powdered sugar and bake for 1 to 2 minutes until sugar caramelizes. Set aside to cool.

Combine the cornstarch, eggs, and ¼ cup of sugar in a medium bowl. Whisk together well. Place milk and remaining sugar in a pot and bring to a boil over high heat. Slowly add the hot milk into the cornstarch mixture while whisking constantly.

Pour the mixture back into the pot. Bring to a boil over medium heat while whisking constantly. Once the mixture has fully thickened, continue cooking and whisking for 1 additional minute to cook out the starch. Remove from heat and stir in the butter, vanilla, and zest. Pour into a medium bowl, press plastic wrap onto the surface of the pudding, and place in the refrigerator to cool.

Cut the puff pastry sheet into 12 (2x4-inch) rectangles. Place one rectangle down on a serving plate, spread some pastry cream on top, lay some blood orange segments on the cream, and top with another puff pastry rectangle. Top with more pastry cream and segments and finally top with another rectangle. Repeat until the remaining puff pastry rectangles are used. Let pastries set up in refrigerator for 30 minutes before serving. Garnish pastries with powdered sugar and let them set up in refrigerator for 30 minutes before serving.

Madeira Baked Dates with Citrus Mascarpone and Honey-Roasted Walnuts

MAKES 6 TO 8 SERVINGS

Madeira Dates:

24 dates, pitted

1 cup Madeira

½ cup sugar

Honey-Roasted Walnuts:

½ cup honey

¼ cup sugar

¼ teaspoon salt

1 cup walnut halves

Citrus Mascarpone:

1 (5-ounce) package mascarpone fresca

1 teaspoon orange zest

These scrumptious dates come alive with flavor when they are baked in sweet Madeira, a fortified Portuguese wine. They are then stuffed with a lively citrus mascarpone and topped with crunchy honey-roasted walnuts. I love serving these with a warm cup of coffee on a chilly winter evening. You'll need a wire rack for this one.

Directions

Preheat oven to 325°F.

Make the dates:

Using a sharp knife, carefully cut through the long side of each date. Pry open the dates and place them cut side down in a 9-inch cake pan.

Place the Madeira and the sugar in a small pot over medium heat and cook until sugar is dissolved. Pour over the dates, cover with foil, and bake for 25 minutes. Remove from oven and pour out the Madeira sauce, reserving it for later. Let the dates cool uncovered in the refrigerator.

Make the walnuts:

Adjust oven temperature to 350°F. Place a wire rack over a foil-lined baking tray and set aside.

Place the honey, sugar, and salt in a small pot over medium heat and simmer for 2 minutes. Stir in the walnuts and continue to simmer for 5 minutes. Strain the mixture through a sieve and spread the walnuts on the wire rack. Bake for 7 minutes until toasted. Remove from oven and let cool completely.

Make the mascarpone:
In a small bowl, stir together the mascarpone and orange zest. Use a small spoon to fill each date, bring the halves together, and arrange the filled dates on a plate.

Use a sharp knife to chop the cooled walnuts into smaller pieces. Press the walnuts onto the tops of the dates. Drizzle with the reserved Madeira sauce.

Cranberry Upside Down Cake

MAKES 1 (9-INCH) CAKE

As you can see, this upside down cake has a loaded top layer of gorgeous cranberries. Their classic tart flavor is perfectly balanced by the sweet gingerbread cake below. This dessert is a nice alternative to mainstream holiday desserts. Served with a simple dollop of whipped cream, this cake is sure to be the start of a new holiday dessert tradition.

Directions

Preheat oven to 350°F. Coat the bottom and sides of a 9-inch round cake pan with 2 tablespoons butter followed by a top coat of pan spray. Set aside.

Add the cranberries, sugar, orange juice, and zest to a medium pot over high heat. Bring the mixture to a boil and cook at a low boil for about 5 minutes until berries burst and sauce thickens. Pour into prepared pan and evenly spread mixture on the bottom.

In a mixer fitted with the paddle attachment, cream ½ cup butter, brown sugar, and vanilla on medium speed until light and fluffy, about 2 minutes. Scrape bowl well. Add the eggs one at a time, mixing well after each addition. Scrape bowl well. Add the flour, baking powder, ginger, cinnamon, and salt. Whisk together the milk, oil, and honey in a small bowl. With the mixer on low, slowly drizzle in the liquids and mix until incorporated. Scrape bowl well and spread batter evenly over the cranberries. Bake until an inserted toothpick comes out clean, about 25 to 30 minutes.

Let cake sit on counter for 10 minutes. Run a paring knife around the edge. Flip out onto a serving plate.

2 tablespoons plus ½ cup
　unsalted butter, soft

3 cups fresh cranberries

½ cup sugar

2 tablespoons orange
　juice

1 tablespoon orange zest

½ cup brown sugar

1 teaspoon vanilla extract

2 large eggs

1½ cups all-purpose flour

1½ teaspoons baking
　powder

1½ teaspoons ground
　ginger

½ teaspoon cinnamon

¼ teaspoon salt

¼ cup whole milk

⅛ cup vegetable oil

⅛ cup honey

Date Pudding Cake
with Vanilla Toffee Sauce

MAKES 1 (9-INCH) ROUND CAKE

Date Pudding Cake:

1 cup deglet noor dates,
  pitted

1 tablespoon rum
  (I prefer Appleton)

1 cup water

2½ ounces unsalted
  butter, soft

⅓ cup sugar

¼ cup brown sugar

2 large eggs

1 cup all-purpose flour

½ teaspoon cinnamon

¼ teaspoon ground
  nutmeg

¼ teaspoon ground
  cloves

¼ teaspoon salt

¾ teaspoon baking soda

Vanilla Toffee Sauce:

⅔ cup heavy cream

1 cup brown sugar

½ cup sugar

½ cup unsalted butter,
  soft

2 tablespoons rum

2 teaspoons vanilla
  extract

When the chill of winter strikes, this date pudding cake is the perfect dessert to make. The rum and spice cake will fill your kitchen with the most tantalizing aroma as it bakes in the oven; the finished cake is then drenched with a warm vanilla toffee sauce, giving it a pudding-like consistency and a dangerously delicious taste. This dessert will undoubtedly warm your soul and fill your tummy at the same time.

Make date pudding cake:

Preheat oven to 325°F. Grease a 9-inch round pan and set aside.

Add the dates and rum to a large bowl. Bring the water to a boil and pour over the dates. Set aside for 10 minutes to soften.

In a mixer fitted to a paddle attachment, beat the butter and sugars on medium speed for 1 minute until light and fluffy. Add the eggs one at a time, beating well after each addition. Scrape bowl well. Add the flour, cinnamon, nutmeg, clove, and salt and mix on low speed until slightly incorporated so you can still see white flour. Purée the dates. (If you don't have a food processor you can use a potato masher or blender, too.) Stir the baking soda into the date mixture and add it to the batter. Mix on medium speed until well blended. Add to the prepared cake pan and bake for 30 to 35 minutes until an inserted toothpick comes out clean. When cake has finished baking, begin making the sauce.

Make vanilla toffee sauce:

Place all the ingredients in a medium pot and bring to a gentle boil over medium heat. Cook for 4 to 5 minutes to thicken sauce, stirring occasionally. Use a toothpick to poke about 30 holes on top of the cake. Slowly pour half of the warm sauce over the cake. Agitate the cake pan slightly to help the sauce soak into the cake. Let cake cool slightly before slicing. Serve cake with the remaining warm toffee sauce.

Banana Bread Pudding

MAKES 1 (1½-QUART) CASSEROLE

Every bite of this delicious bread pudding is loaded with chunks of fresh bananas. It can be baked in a large casserole dish or in individual ramekins for more formal meals. Ice cream, crème anglaise, and caramel sauce all make delicious toppings to this amazing bread pudding.

Directions

Preheat oven to 350°F. Place the cubed bread in a large bowl and set aside.

Grease the bottom and sides of a 1½-quart baking dish (or individual ramekins if you prefer) with the butter. Add 1 tablespoon of sugar to coat the dish. Set aside. Add 6 tablespoons of sugar and the cream to a medium pot and bring to a boil. In a large bowl, whisk remaining sugar, eggs, yolks, vanilla, and salt together. Slowly pour the hot cream into the egg mixture, whisking continuously. Place a mesh strainer over the bread bowl and pour the custard base through the sieve. Stir the bread mixture so that all the pieces are evenly coated with the custard. Cover the bowl with plastic and let sit for 2 minutes.

Break up the bananas into chunks with the back of a fork. Gently fold them into the bread pudding mixture and transfer to the prepared dish. Bake for 20 to 25 minutes or until the top springs back when gently tapped.

5½ ounces white bread, cubed

1 tablespoon unsalted butter, soft

12 tablespoons sugar

2 cups half and half

3 large eggs

2 large egg yolks

2 teaspoons vanilla extract

¼ teaspoon salt

2 large bananas, ripe

Banana Boats

2 large bananas, ripe
¼ cup chunky peanut
butter
¼ cup chopped semi-
sweet chocolate
Sugar for sprinkling

This is a really fun dessert to make *and* serve. They always seem to cause an uproar when I bring them to the table. This recipe showcases the classic pairing of peanut butter and chocolate. Other fun "stuffings" include almond butter, marshmallows, shredded coconut, and butterscotch chips.

Directions

Preheat oven to 350°F. Line a sheet tray with parchment paper and set aside.

Use a sharp knife to slice the bananas lengthwise. Carefully remove the banana halves from their peels. Working with one half at a time, cut bite-size slices while keeping the banana intact. Spread a tablespoon of peanut butter into each peel, lay the bananas on top, and place on the prepared sheet tray. Sprinkle some sugar on top followed by the chopped chocolate. Bake for 10 minutes. Serve immediately.

Lemon Grahams

MAKES 1 (8-INCH) SQUARE PAN

This is my farm-to-table version of lemon bars. I've never been a huge fan of the traditional lemon bar; just too buttery and one-dimensional for me. These bars, however, are far more interesting thanks to the soft graham layer that provides a rustic flavor and chewy texture. I like to keep these bars in the refrigerator and serve them chilled.

Make the crust:

Preheat oven to 350°F. Grease an 8-inch square pan and line the bottom with parchment paper. Set aside.

In a large bowl, stir together the graham crumbs, sugar, and flour. Add the melted butter and mix well with your hands. Transfer to prepared pan and press onto the bottom. Bake for 15 minutes, rotating halfway. Crust will be a dark golden brown.

Make the filling:

In a large bowl, whisk the sugars, flour, and salt together. Add the butter and cream. Whisk in the eggs, lemon juice, zest, and vanilla. Pour over crust and carefully place in oven. Bake for 25 minutes, rotating halfway. Reduce oven temperature to 325°F and bake for 8 minutes more. Remove from oven and let cool completely in refrigerator before inverting and slicing. Garnish with powdered sugar before serving.

Crust:

1 cup graham crumbs

1 tablespoon sugar

1 tablespoon all-purpose flour

2 ounces salted butter, melted

Filling:

½ cup sugar

¼ cup brown sugar

½ tablespoon all-purpose flour

¼ teaspoon salt

2 tablespoons unsalted butter, melted

2 tablespoons heavy cream

2 large eggs

2 tablespoons lemon juice

1 teaspoon lemon zest

1 teaspoon vanilla extract

Creamy Rice Pudding

MAKES 2-3 SERVINGS

3 cups whole milk

¼ cup sugar plus 2
   tablespoons sugar

1 orange slice

½ cinnamon stick

¼ cup short-grain rice

½ teaspoon cornstarch

1 large egg

1 teaspoon vanilla extract

This creamy and delicious rice pudding is flavored with a hint of citrus and cinnamon. It's pure comfort food that is a nice change from the typical array of pies, cakes, and ice cream that top many dessert tables. If you prefer your pudding to be less creamy, add a little water at the very end to thin it out.

Directions

Combine the milk, ¼ cup sugar, orange slice, and cinnamon stick in a medium pot and bring to a boil over high heat. Add the rice. Stirring occasionally, simmer until rice is tender, about 30 minutes. Remove and discard orange slice and cinnamon stick.

   In a small bowl, whisk the cornstarch and 2 tablespoons sugar. Whisk in the egg. Add mixture to the rice and bring the rice back to a boil for 1 minute. Remove from heat and fold in the vanilla. If serving chilled, portion pudding into serving cups and press plastic wrap onto the tops to prevent skin from forming.

Coconut Cream Pie

MAKES 1 (9-INCH) PIE

Crust:

2 cups crushed vanilla
   wafers

¼ cup unsalted butter,
   melted

Filling:

2 coconuts

2½ cups reduced fat milk

1 cup sugar

4 large egg yolks

6 tablespoons all-
   purpose flour

1 tablespoon cornstarch

¼ teaspoon salt

3 tablespoons unsalted
   butter, soft

1 tablespoon vanilla
   extract

Topping:

1½ cups heavy cream,
   chilled

2 tablespoons sugar

1 teaspoon vanilla extract

According to the Pacific Island Agroforestry, a mature coconut tree can produce as much as 80 coconuts annually and may continue to bear fruit for many, many years. This explains why fresh coconut, whose peak season is listed as winter, is available year-round. While it takes a good amount of effort to extract the meat from a coconut, the fresh, natural flavor it gives this pie far exceeds that of store-bought sweetened coconut.

Make the crust:

Combine wafers and butter in a medium bowl and mix well. Transfer to a 9-inch pie plate and press onto bottom and sides. Place in refrigerator to chill.

Make the filling:

Use a nail and hammer to pierce the softest eye on the coconut. Drain the coconut water and store it in the refrigerator for sipping later. Separate the meat from the coconut shell using a small paring knife. Cut the meat from one of the coconuts into small pieces and place them in a pot. Finely grate the meat from the other coconut, place in a zippered bag, and keep in refrigerator for later. Add the milk to the pot and bring it to a boil over high heat. Remove from heat, cover, and let steep for 20 minutes.

Strain the milk into a large bowl and discard the coconut pieces. Return ⅔ of the milk to the pot and stir in ½ cup sugar. Warm over medium heat.

Whisk the reserved milk, the remaining ½ cup sugar, yolks, flour, cornstarch, and salt. Slowly whisk in the yolk mixture to the milk in the pot. Bring to a full boil for 1 minute, stirring constantly. Remove from heat and stir in the butter and vanilla. Fold in half of the grated coconut. Transfer to the pie shell and press plastic wrap onto the top to prevent a skin from forming. Let chill completely in refrigerator for at least 4 hours.

Make the topping:

In a mixer fitted with the whip attachment, beat the cream, sugar, and vanilla to medium-stiff peaks. Spread over cooled filling and top with remaining grated coconut.

Brown Butter Banana Soufflé

MAKES 4 SERVINGS

This soufflé is an exquisite way to showcase the much-loved banana. Combining light-as-air texture with sweet banana flavor, this soufflé will disappear within seconds because it's so delectable. As with most banana dessert recipes, make sure to use very ripe bananas.

Soft, unsalted butter and sugar for coating ramekins

2 tablespoons unsalted butter, soft

2 large bananas, very ripe

2 teaspoons all-purpose flour

6 tablespoons sugar

4 large egg whites, room temperature

Directions

Preheat oven to 375°F. Coat the bottom and sides of 4 (1 cup) ramekins with butter. Add some sugar to the ramekins to coat. Set aside.

Bring butter to a boil in a small pot over medium heat. Stir the butter with a rubber spatula and continue boiling until brown bits begin to appear. Remove from heat and add to a blender, along with the bananas, flour, and 4 tablespoons sugar. Blend a few seconds or until bananas are puréed. Transfer to a clean bowl and set aside.

In a mixer fitted with the whip attachment, beat the egg whites until frothy. Slowly add 2 tablespoons of sugar and beat to medium-stiff peaks. Fold the whites into the banana mixture in three portions. Use a small spoon to portion out the batter into the prepared ramekins. Bake for 15 minutes. Serve immediately.

Kiwi Coconut Pops

MAKES 3-4 SERVINGS

1 cup fresh coconut
    water (from 1 large
    coconut)
3 kiwis, very ripe
2 teaspoons agave

This is a fun dessert to make with kids. It uses fresh coconut water straight from a coconut. Look for coconuts that sound full of water when shaken and make sure to use the ripest kiwi available. Sweetened with agave, these nutritious pops are loaded with vitamin E and electrolytes.

Directions

Use a nail and hammer to pierce the softest eye on the coconut. Drain the coconut water into a measuring cup and pour 1 cup's worth in a blender.

Use a sharp knife to cut off the ends of the kiwi and slice off the skin; leave as much flesh as possible. Cut them into quarters and add to the blender.

Add the agave and mix on low speed for a few seconds—that's it! Don't crush the kiwi seeds or your pops will taste bitter. Pour into molds and freeze for at least 4 hours or until completely frozen.

Ruby Red Grapefruit Pie

MAKES 1 (9-INCH) PIE

This pie does a remarkable job at showcasing the wonderfully sweet tang of fresh winter grapefruit. Segments of fruit are layered with a strawberry-cranberry gelée and sweetened cream cheese. The sweet-salty pretzel crust takes this pie over the top.

Directions

Preheat oven to 350°F. Grease a 9-inch pie pan (or springform pan) with pan spray and set aside.

Hull and halve the strawberries and toss them with ¼ cup sugar in a small bowl. Let sit undisturbed to macerate while you prepare the crust.

In a medium bowl, combine the crushed pretzels and 3 tablespoons sugar. Add the melted butter and mix well. Press the mixture onto the bottom of the prepared pan. Bake for 10 minutes. Remove from oven and place in freezer to cool.

In a mixer fitted with the paddle attachment, beat cream cheese on medium speed until smooth. Add the sugar and beat on high speed for 5 minutes. Remove crust from freezer and evenly spread cream cheese mixture on top. Return to freezer to set up.

Line a sheet tray with some paper towels. Using a sharp knife, cut the skin off of the grapefruits. Cut out segments of grapefruit and arrange them on the towels to dry. Set aside.

Add the macerated strawberries and cranberry juice to a blender and purée well. Strain the juice into a small pot and discard pulp. Place gelatin in a small bowl and add ⅓ cup of the juice. Stir to incorporate and let sit 5 minutes to soften.

Warm the remaining juice in the pot over low heat. When lukewarm to touch, remove from heat and stir in the gelatin mixture. Remove pie from freezer. Arrange the grapefruit segments on top. Slowly pour the gelée juice over the segments. Place pie in refrigerator for at least 2 hours before serving.

8 ounces strawberries

¼ cup sugar plus 3 tablespoons sugar

5 ounces pretzel sticks, finely crushed

¾ cup unsalted butter, melted

1 (8-ounce) package cream cheese, room temperature

⅓ cup sugar

2 Ruby Red grapefruits

⅓ cup cranberry juice

1½ teaspoons powdered gelatin

Carrot Raisin Walnut Cake

MAKES 1 (10-INCH) BUNDT CAKE

3–4 large carrots, peeled

1½ cups raisins

2 cups boiling water

3 cups all-purpose flour

1 ½ cups chopped walnuts

1 tablespoon baking soda

1 tablespoon cinnamon

1 teaspoon salt

4 large eggs

2 cups sugar

1½ cups vegetable oil

1 cup crushed pineapple,
    drained

1 tablespoon vanilla
    extract

Winter is peak season for carrots. Look for ones with smooth skin, no splits, and bright leafy tops. This dense and flavorful cake is packed with walnuts, carrots, raisins, and pineapple. Its beautiful presentation is so striking you'll find it hard to cut that first slice, but it'll be well worth it.

Directions

Preheat oven to 325°F. Grease a 10-inch Bundt pan. Use a peeler to cut 8 long, thin strips from one of the carrots. Line the Bundt pan with the strips and trim them if necessary. Set aside pan.

Shred 1½ cups of carrots and set aside. Place the raisins in a bowl. Pour the boiling water over the raisins and set aside to plump.

Combine the flour, walnuts, baking soda, cinnamon, and salt in a large bowl and set aside. Add the eggs, sugar, and oil to a mixer fitted with the paddle attachment and mix on low speed until blended. Add the pineapple, shredded carrots, and vanilla. Mix until incorporated. Scrape bowl. Add the dry ingredients and the drained raisins and mix for 1 minute. Use a large ice cream scoop to transfer batter into the prepared pan.

Bake for 1 hour and 15 minutes or until an inserted toothpick comes out clean. Cool completely before inverting onto serving platter.

Tangerine Flan

MAKES 1 (9X5X3-INCH) FLAN

Tangerines are a winter fruit but their season can extend into spring. Sweeter and smaller in size than oranges, tangerines have pebbly skin and are easy to peel. This recipe uses 2 to 3 tangerines. If you have extras, serve them fresh alongside the flan. Served warm or cold, this smooth and creamy flan with delightful citrus notes is always a hit.

Directions

Preheat oven to 350°F. Place a large oblong pan filled with 1-inch deep water in the oven for your water bath. Set a 9x5x3-inch loaf pan on the counter.

Place half the sugar in a small, heavy pot over medium heat. Slowly drizzle in ¼ cup water. Gently swirl the pot to blend the sugar and water. Once the syrup is clear, let it boil undisturbed until it begins to darken, about 8 to 10 minutes. Gently swirl the pot to evenly caramelize the syrup. Once dark amber is achieved, pour all of the syrup into the loaf pan and carefully tilt the pan to coat the bottom and sides. Set aside to cool.

Combine the milks, tangerine juice, and zest in a medium pot. Place over high heat and heat until just steaming. Whisk the eggs and yolk with the remaining sugar in a large bowl. Slowly strain the hot milk into the eggs and whisk until sugar is dissolved. Whisk in the vanilla.

Pour the custard base into the prepared pan. Place in the water bath and bake for 1½ to 2 hours, or until custard is set (look for the Jell-O jiggle). Let set up at least 6 hours or overnight. To unmold, dip the loaf pan briefly into hot water, loosen the edges with a sharp knife, and invert onto serving platter.

1½ cups sugar

¼ cup water

1 (12-ounce) can evaporated milk

1 cup whole milk

½ cup tangerine juice

2 tablespoons tangerine zest

4 large eggs and 1 large yolk

½ teaspoon vanilla extract

Meyer Lemon Rosemary Cake with Almond Crust

MAKES 1 (9X5X3-INCH) CAKE

Crust:

1 tablespoon unsalted
   butter, soft

½ cup sliced almonds

1 tablespoon sugar

Cake:

1¼ cups sugar

½ cup unsalted butter, soft

1 teaspoon Meyer lemon
   zest

2 large eggs

1½ cups all-purpose flour

½ teaspoon rosemary,
   finely chopped

⅛ teaspoon baking soda

⅛ teaspoon baking
   powder

⅛ teaspoon salt

⅓ cup plus 1 tablespoon
   buttermilk

Syrup:

¼ cup Meyer lemon juice

1 teaspoon sugar

Combined with a crunchy almond crust, this soft cake is super flavorful and delicious. This eye-catching loaf beautifully captures the fragrance and flavor of Meyer lemons. You'll need 2 lemons to make this recipe. The lemons' zest is added to the cake batter while the juice is poured over the baked cake, allowing the sweet flavor of Meyer lemons to infuse throughout.

Make the crust:

Preheat oven to 350°F. Coat the bottom and sides of a 9x5x3-inch loaf pan with 1 tablespoon butter. Sprinkle the almonds in a single layer on the bottom as well as three-quarters way up the sides. Sprinkle the sugar evenly over the almonds and set pan aside.

Make the cake:

In a mixer fitted with the paddle attachment, cream the sugar, butter, and zest on medium speed for 1 minute until light and fluffy. Add eggs one at a time, mixing well after each addition. Scrape the bowl well to ensure ingredients are incorporated. Add the flour, rosemary, baking soda, baking powder, and salt. Turn mixer to low speed and slowly pour in the buttermilk. Scrape bowl well and transfer batter to the prepared pan. Bake 50 to 60 minutes or until an inserted toothpick comes out clean.

Make the syrup:

While cake bakes, squeeze 2 Meyer lemons to get ¼ cup juice. Combine the juice with 1 teaspoon of sugar in a small pot over low heat. Stir until sugar is dissolved. Set aside. When cake is done, poke holes with a toothpick all over the top. Slowly pour the sweetened juice over the cake. Let cool completely before flipping out onto serving plate.

Clementines in Spiced Syrup
MAKES 5-6 SERVINGS

This is an easy way to dress up clementines. The segments are soaked in a sugar syrup and deliciously flavored with ginger, cardamom, and anise. After soaking the fruit for a couple hours, break up the segments and serve alone or as a garnish on desserts. Try serving them with a dollop of whipped cream and my Meyer Lemon Rosemary Cake on page 168.

Directions

Combine water, sugar, Cointreau, and ginger slices in a small pot and stir to incorporate. Coarsely grind the cardamom, cinnamon, and anise in a mortar and pestle. Add the spices to the pot and bring to a boil over high heat. Reduce heat and let simmer for 10 minutes until fragrant and syrupy. Let cool in the freezer while you prep the clementines.

Peel the clementines and remove as much white pith as possible. You can leave them whole or break up the segments. Place them in a small bowl and strain the spiced syrup over them. Chill for at least 2 hours before serving.

1 cup water
½ cup sugar
1 tablespoon Cointreau
1 (1-inch) piece of fresh
 ginger, thinly sliced
3 cardamom pods
1 stick cinnamon
½ teaspoon anise seeds
1 pound (about 5 or 6)
 clementines

Meyer Lemon Cream Puffs

MAKES ABOUT 30 CREAM PUFFS

Cream:

1 cup sugar

¾ cup unsalted butter

¾ cup Meyer lemon juice

2 tablespoons Meyer
   lemon zest

9 large egg yolks

1½ cups heavy whipping
   cream

Fresh strawberry slices
   (optional)

Powdered sugar, for
   garnish

Puffs:

1 cup reduced-fat milk

½ cup unsalted butter

1 tablespoon Meyer
   lemon zest

2 teaspoons sugar

¼ teaspoon salt

1 cup all-purpose flour

4 large eggs

Meyer lemons start appearing in December and last through April. Look for ones with a slightly orange skin—a sign that it is fully ripe. I love making custards out of Meyer lemons because they have such a unique flavor and yield more juice than commercial lemons. These cream puffs are light, airy, and delicious. I like to add a layer of farm fresh strawberries, but this is optional.

Make the cream:

Combine half of the sugar, butter, lemon juice, and zest in a medium pot. Bring to a boil over medium heat, stirring occasionally. Meanwhile, whisk the egg yolks with the remaining sugar in a bowl. Slowly pour half of the hot lemon juice mixture to the yolks, whisking constantly. Return the tempered egg mixture to the pot over low-medium heat. Continue cooking, stirring constantly, until the custard boils for 10 seconds. Remove from heat and strain into a shallow container or bowl. Press plastic wrap directly onto the surface of the custard. Place in refrigerator to cool while you make the puffs.

Make the puffs:

Preheat oven to 425°F. Line two sheet trays with parchment paper and set aside.

Combine the milk, butter, zest, sugar, and salt in a medium pot over high heat. Once mixture comes to a boil, reduce the heat, add the flour all at once, and stir briskly for 2 minutes to dry out the batter. Transfer the batter to a mixer fitted with the paddle attachment. Mix on medium speed for a few minutes to cool the batter. Reduce speed to low and add the eggs one at a time, mixing for 30 seconds after each addition. Transfer batter to a piping bag with a smooth tip and pipe small mounds about 1-inch apart. Bake for 10 minutes. Reduce oven temperature to 350°F and bake for 15 to 25 minutes more until the puffs sound hollow when tapped on the bottom. Remove puffs from oven and let cool on counter.

Whip the heavy cream to medium-stiff peaks in a mixer fitted with the whip attachment. Fold the cooled lemon custard into the cream with a whisk.

Cut the tops of the puffs off with a serrated knife. Fill the bottoms with the lemon cream, layer a couple strawberry slices if desired, and place tops on. Place in refrigerator for at least 30 minutes to set. Garnish with powdered sugar before serving.

Acknowledgments

🍓 To my wonderful editorial team, Nicole Frail and Nicole Mele at Skyhorse Publishing, thank you for your enthusiasm for this project and helping me create a cookbook of which I am so proud. I truly believe there aren't any nicer editors in the world.

🍓 To my agent Deborah Ritchken, thank you for continuing to find me opportunities I love.

🍓 To the farmers and vendors at all the markets I frequently visit, thank you for putting up with all my questions.

🍓 To my husband, G, thank you for being my secret weapon and loving me like no other.

Index

Conversion Charts

METRIC AND IMPERIAL CONVERSIONS
(These conversions are rounded for convenience)

Ingredient	Cups/Tablespoons/Teaspoons	Ounces	Grams/Milliliters
Butter	1 cup = 16 tablespoons = 2 sticks	8 ounces	230 grams
Cheese, shredded	1 cup	4 ounces	110 grams
Cream cheese	1 tablespoon	0.5 ounce	14.5 grams
Cornstarch	1 tablespoon	0.3 ounce	8 grams
Flour, all-purpose	1 cup/1 tablespoon	4.5 ounces/0.3 ounce	125 grams/8 grams
Flour, whole wheat	1 cup	4 ounces	120 grams
Fruit, dried	1 cup	4 ounces	120 grams
Fruits or veggies, chopped	1 cup	5 to 7 ounces	145 to 200 grams
Fruits or veggies, puréed	1 cup	8.5 ounces	245 grams
Honey, maple syrup, or corn syrup	1 tablespoon	.75 ounce	20 grams
Liquids: cream, milk, water, or juice	1 cup	8 fluid ounces	240 milliliters
Oats	1 cup	5.5 ounces	150 grams
Salt	1 teaspoon	0.2 ounce	6 grams
Spices: cinnamon, cloves, ginger, or nutmeg (ground)	1 teaspoon	0.2 ounce	5 milliliters
Sugar, brown, firmly packed	1 cup	7 ounces	200 grams
Sugar, white	1 cup/1 tablespoon	7 ounces/0.5 ounce	200 grams/12.5 grams
Vanilla extract	1 teaspoon	0.2 ounce	4 grams

Fahrenheit	Celsius	Gas Mark
225°	110°	¼
250°	120°	½
275°	140°	1
300°	150°	2
325°	160°	3
350°	180°	4
375°	190°	5
400°	200°	6
425°	220°	7
450°	230°	8